YOUR IDENTITY IN CHRIST

BY: VERONICA EVANS

©2016 by Veronica Evans

Published by V K & Z Publishing Company

Printed in the United States of America

All rights reserved. The copyright laws of the United States of America protect this book. No part of this publication may be reproduced or stored in a retrieval system for commercial gain or profit. No part of this publication may be stored electronically or otherwise transmitted in any form or by any means—for example, electronic, photocopy, recording-- without written permission of the publisher.

Unless otherwise identified, Scripture quotations are from the New King James Version, copyright © Thomas Nelson, Inc. Used by permission. All rights reserved.

Scripture notations identified Complete Jewish Bible or CJB are from COMPLETE JEWISH BIBLE © 1998 by David H. Stern, published by Jewish New Testament Publications, Inc. Used by permission. All rights reserved.

Scripture quotations identified KJV are from The Full Life Study Bible-King James Version ©1992 by Life Publishers International. Used by permission. All rights reserved.

Scripture quotations identified ESV from the English Standard Version free online Bible Study Tool, offered by www.Blueletterbible.com. Used by permission. All rights reserved

Scripture notations identified NLT are from the Life Application Study Bible-New Living Translation, ©1996 by, 2004 by Tyndale House Publishers, Inc. Used by permission. All rights reserved.

ISBN: 978-0-9978733-0-6

Library of Congress Cataloging-in-Publication Data

Edited by Yvonne Perry Consulting Services, LLC, Raleigh, NC
Manager@perryconsultingservices.com

Cover design by J. Alexander Online

This book is dedicated to my husband, Kirby Evans, my two beautiful children Zion and Moriah, my incredible mother, father, and siblings. You have all taught me the value of family and graciously given me the space to be who God created me to be.

Table of Contents

Introduction 1

Chapter One
Fearfully and Wonderfully Made in His Image 4

Chapter Two
DNA and Your Royal Bloodline 17

Chapter Three
Come Out of Her 34

Chapter Four
In Christ 59

Chapter Five
Sonship: Your Kingdom Inheritance 74

Chapter Six
Kings and Priests of God 92

Chapter Seven
Kingdom Ambassadors 107

Chapter Eight
Walk In Your Kingdom Authority and Win 118

Prayer of Activation 129

References 131

INTRODUCTION

Within this past year, Holy Spirit has been taking me on a journey to discover my identity. He has shown me just how limited and myopic my scope has been regarding who I am in the Kingdom of God. As I have embraced this heavenly journey, I am convinced today more than ever that today's society, and the body of Christ, are struggling due to a serious identity crisis. Social media is inundated with super thin models and offer all kinds of cosmetic remedies to alter one's outward appearance, but you rarely find instructions on how to live life from the inside out. For some strange reason, we have come to believe that if we change our outward appearance, this change takes place inwardly as well. Not! We have been somehow blinded to the reality that spiritual life supersedes physical life. If we're not careful, we can live our entire lives trying to find out who we are externally and looking to other people to validate just to come to the end of the road and conclude as Solomon did, that all is vanity and a grasping for the wind (Eccl. 1:14).

I recently returned from a mission's trip to the cities of Accra and Kumasi, in Ghana, Africa. When seeking the Lord about what to teach while there, He led me to teach on the very subject that He has been redefining for me. In this book I will communicate to you the revelation given to me, along with various scriptures and experiences about my discovery. Also, while in my prayer time during the early part of last year and while petitioning the Lord for a specific need, the Lord said to me, "You are a king and priest in My Kingdom; walk as such in the earth." God's reply and directive hit me like a lightning bolt, and suddenly I realized that obviously I was unaware of who I was to Abba Father.

Additionally, I will refer to God as Abba at times. I love using the name "Abba" (Matthew 14:36; Romans 8:15; Galatians 4:6) which means "Father" because it signifies relationship and sonship. Jesus instructed us in Matthew 6:9 to pray to, "Our Father." The term "Abba" does not lessen who God is in His nature; on the contrary, it displays His loving desire to be our Father and expresses our longing to be His children. There are times that our various religious backgrounds prohibit us from really understanding how Abba wants us to see Him. He's not a tyrant ready to release swift judgment on us! He's not too holy that He's unapproachable, although I do believe there is a right way and attitude to approach Him. He's not this angry God who doesn't love His children. No. He's a loving Father with a loving Son and a loving Spirit who wants to enjoy precious fellowship with the very people He created. This is what makes Him so different from any other god, who are really not gods at all, worshipped and exalted by man. Our God, Yahweh, is alive! He interacts and intervenes with and for His children. He counsels and leads us throughout our daily lives. He tells us things to come and sets us on course with our respective destinies. Yes. He loves us more than we know and wants us to live life with purpose.

The passion of my heart and the assignment set before me is that of revealing your identity in Christ, as a child of the King. I want every believer reading this book to KNOW who you are, to whom you belong, and the rights you possess. Here's an example. Prince Charles could not enjoy the benefits of being a prince until he knew and understood that he was a child of royalty. Once he understood this indelible truth, he could begin to walk in his designated role with confidence, and exercise the inherited rights of a prince.

This book is for the radical…the game changer. It is for the believer who is tired of living beneath what Jesus died for. It is for those who are ready to walk in their respective kingdom positions with divine authority. This book is for the mature believer who understands the duty of their call and ready to advance further territory for the Kingdom of God.

Lastly, I want this book to be an awakening for those who have been spiritually asleep. I pray it will remove the blinders of religion so that your eyes will be anointed with the eye salve of Jesus (Revelation 3:18). To all who know there's more to this life than what you have experienced in the past or experiencing now….this book is for you!

As you read Your Identity in Christ, be sure to journal what you sense Holy Spirit speaking to your heart. Journaling is extremely important to God, so be intentional about writing down impressions, dreams and visions, and record songs you may hear along the way. Purpose in your heart to live according to what and who the Bible says you are and remain resolute in refuting any negative words about your identity.

CHAPTER ONE

Fearfully and Wonderfully Made in His Image

> "I will praise You, for I am fearfully and wonderfully made; Marvelous are Your works, And that my soul knows very well."
> Psalm 139:14

Today I want to empower you! I want to help open your eyes and bring clarity about who you are in the Kingdom of God. If you're like me, you have spent a lot of time trying to change who you are. Let me first say that change is good if it is in agreement with the character of God and His Word. There's absolutely nothing wrong with making improvements. Every singer wants to sing better. Every author wants to write better. Every manager wants to manage better. I actually prefer to refer to these as enhancements because enhancements do not change the whole of who you are; they simply improve the quality of your gifts and skill levels and advance them to a higher level.

We all know that when we became born again, there were things and ways about our old nature that had to change or be crucified. Some of these changes happened immediately, while many changes have been gradual. There are certain characteristics that you have been graced with that are intended to amplify your true identity. I have a strong voice and because I took the time to enhance my voice through practice and training, it has been fashioned to sing on a certain level. I am not saying that just because you train certain gifts and abilities that you will become a professional, and although some will, the goal is to make your gift or talent more proficient.

So let's begin with WHOSE you are. Everyone has a biological mother and father, but the truth is, we existed in the realm of the spirit long before our mothers and fathers ever knew each other. I know it may seem difficult for some to comprehend because in our present state, we have no recollection of our prior-earth existence. In Jeremiah 1:5 the Lord says, "Before I formed you in the womb I knew you; Before you were born I sanctified you; I ordained you a prophet to the nations." God clearly and definitively told Jeremiah that before HE created or formed him in his mother's womb, He knew him and was acquainted with him. So let's first understand that we were spirit beings long before we were earth beings. So there you have it. Out with the Big Bang Theory and the Evolution rhetoric! God clearly says that before He formed us inside of our mother's womb, not only did He know us but He set us apart for a specific work, then formed us in the womb and commissioned us to carry out the purpose for which He had set us apart for. Life for us did not begin solely at conception as some believe.

So what does this mean? It means that you are not an accident! You are not helpless, hopeless individuals. You are not the "oops" of a one-night stand. Your loving Father knew when to design and create you and place you in your mother's womb. He knew exactly when to place you in the womb and set you on course to fulfill His purpose and plan. Now I know that some of you may be thinking that if God is so loving, then why would He place you in a family where there was abuse or neglect or dysfunction? Well, let me say this. Every family has dysfunction. We are all born into sin and shaped in iniquity but regardless of what family we were placed in, Abba and His angelic hosts watched over us despite the depravities we experienced during our childhood years.

In order to enjoy life to its fullest measure, the life that Jesus promised in John 10:10, we must know to whom we belong. If we belong to the King of Kings, then there is a certain posture we must embrace, a certain authority, a certain mindset, a certain understanding that we must grasp and live out. If you limit your existence to your earthly mother and father alone, there are some advantages in this life that you will clearly miss.

David said that it was God who fashioned his innermost being and knit him together in his mother's womb, according to Psalm 139:14. At the thought of this incomprehensible act, David began to thank God for the revelation of such knowledge. He was so encapsulated by this knowledge that he began to declare how he was awesomely and wonderfully made by God the Creator. Another way to say it is, "You are an awesome wonder!"

If you will pause to meditate and ponder on the fact that the God of the universe took His precious, divine hands and meticulously handcrafted every one of His children, designed a womb tailor-made for them, wrote His purposes in their DNA, recorded each day of their lives in His book, and sent them off to carry out His purposes, it will astound you. Such knowledge is too wonderful to behold! You, my friend, have been uniquely created. There is no one else like you. There has never been and neither will there ever be another you! Out of all of the billions of people living upon the face of the earth today, God created you as His awesome wonder! Selah!

Man has a special place in the heart of God that no other species on the planet has....not even the angels. God handcrafted you and me. He created an earth suit for us to wear, allowed us to be a part of His redeemed humanity, gave us a timeframe to complete our assignments, and will soon call us back home to give an account for the work we've accomplished here on planet earth. You, my brothers and sisters, were made by Yahuwah (the Lord's real name). You belong to a higher Kingdom. You are citizens of a divine Kingdom in another realm. Paul said in Philippians 3:20-21, "For our citizenship is in Heaven, from which we also eagerly wait for the Savior, the Lord Jesus Christ, who will transform our lowly body that it may be conformed to His glorious body, according to the working by which He is able even to subdue all things to Himself." The Complete Jewish Bible says it this way, "But we are citizens of Heaven, and it is from there that we expect a Deliverer, the Lord Yeshua the Messiah. He will change the bodies we have in this humble state and make them like his glorious body, using the power which enables him to bring everything under his control." Did you get that? We are citizens of Heaven. Heaven is our reporting station. It is where we are from and where we belong. Once your assignment is done here on earth, it is Jesus who will provide you with a glorified body suitable to inherit His heavenly Kingdom and you will live forever with Him! Hallelujah!

You are the creation of an awesome God. David said in Psalm 139:2, "You know my sitting down and my rising up; You understand my thought afar off." David understood that it was Yahuwah who created him. He understood that because God was his Divine Creator, God knew every intricate, intimate detail about him. He knew that God knew his uprising and his sitting down and all of his thoughts. If we, like David, can grasp the reality that God knows what we're thinking all the time, we would guard our thoughts more carefully and cause them to be more God-focused. Another interesting reality is that Jesus could always perceive the thoughts of man, so thoughts are very powerful in the realm of the spirit. God knows what you think about Him and what you think about yourself. He wants your thoughts about you to agree with His thoughts about you. David knew that it didn't matter what he did or where he went, Abba Father not only knew where he was, but also knew what he was thinking.

The Lord has taken me through various events where I have had to abandon my thoughts about certain ideas and people. Because we have the tendency to see through the eyes of flesh, it will obstruct our view of perceiving things and people accurately. It's amazing to know that even as babies, God sees us as complete. In the realm of the spirit, we are already complete in Him. Although there is a process that we go through, it still does not hinder God's ability to see us as complete. If God sees you as complete, then you cannot become stuck or sidetracked when you make mistakes or miss the mark. The hope is that you will learn from your mistakes, get back on track and keep moving forward. It is the enemy's desire to keep you wallowing in sin or reflecting on bad situations or past traumas. God provided a means of escape and atonement through Jesus Christ, and your acceptance and continued obedience of Him keeps you on the right path.

Falling down is not the same as falling out. As Christians, we will fall down; however, as is the case for disciplined, determined athletes, Christians know how to get up, regain momentum and focus, and get back in the game. Contrarily, when you fall out, you are out of the game and that is never God's intention for any of His children.

If you have been saved for any amount of time, then you may have heard the terms omniscient, omnipresent, and omnipotent. All three refer to God alone, because only He can be all three at all times or any given time. This is one reason why David could say that the Father knew his thoughts from afar and his uprising and sitting down. Our God knows what we think and He knows how we feel (Matt. 4:22). Not only does Jesus know what we feel, but He also feels what we feel according to Hebrews 4:15. Jesus can relate to our hurts and frustrations. There is nothing hidden from Him. Job said in Job 37:16 that God is perfect in knowledge. There is nothing hidden from His all-seeing eyes. He stands outside the corridors of time and gazes intently upon the doings of humanity.

Abba is also omnipresent which means He is everywhere at the same time. David stated in Psalm 139 verses 7-9 that there was nowhere he could go that God would not be. Jesus said in Matthew 28:20b, "And lo I am with you always, even to the end of the age." There's no height or depth that you can run to that will conceal you from the all-seeing eyes of God. His presence is always there. His eyes run to and fro throughout the whole earth to show Himself strong on your behalf (2 Chronicles 16:9). His beauty is seen everywhere. The Heaven's declare His glory and display His handiwork. The angels sing of His praise, and the universe bows at His majesty! His heavenly hosts are all around you carrying out the plans of your Creator. His presence is felt and seen everywhere you turn. His deeds are vividly displayed and inadvertently enjoyed. Our God is an awesome God and you are the object of His affection.

Thirdly, our God is omnipotent, meaning He is all-powerful. There is no power on earth or in the cosmos greater than the power of Yahuwah. While the enemy has some power, he is NOT ALL-POWERFUL! Psalm 29:4 says, "The voice of the Lord is powerful; the voice of the Lord is full of majesty." Did you read that? His voice is powerful and full of majesty, which means that His voice is beautiful and full of royal power. The term royal denotes something or someone from a kingly lineage. The Kingdom of God is not a democracy like we have in the United States but it is governed by a monarch, King Jesus. There is greatness and a splendor in His voice.

According to Hebrews 4:12, we also know that His word is quick and powerful and sharper than any two-edged sword. The word of our God is alive and active and creative and life-giving and life-breathing. When you are born again, the Word provided the way of salvation and the Ruah HaKodesh (Holy Spirit), the breath of God, came to dwell in your heart through faith. Yahuwah's Word is more powerful than anyone else's words. God spoke and creation happened. No Big Bang. Abba speaks and people are healed, lives are restored, souls are saved, mountains tremble, and the dead come to life!

    You must accept who you are regardless of how society or your family attempts to define or redefine you. Regardless of how you feel about your abilities or your inabilities, the Creator made you. When you love yourself as the person God created, you will begin to understand His love in a different way and start to thrive in your Kingdom purposes. There's power in knowing! I once heard someone say that God puts His "super" on our "natural". When you understand that you are beautiful in the eyes of Abba, you won't need validation from anyone else. When you understand that you have been wired for success, you won't seek to be like everyone else. When you understand that you have a Savior who is the King of Kings, you won't settle for little. Why am I saying all of this? I want you to change how you see yourself. I want you to look through the mirror of the Bible and see the real reflection of you. I want you to stop pretending. I want you to stop wanting to look and be like someone else and be you…the real you!

    I had someone say something amazingly powerful to me after encountering two shaky pregnancies. They were asking me if we were planning to have a third child and I emphatically replied, "No." The reason I responded so assertively and quickly was because although my first pregnancy resulted in an 8-pound bouncing baby boy, it was also the result of

5 months of modified activity to include no driving. The person's response to my answer was, "Why not?" This person went on to say that children are eternal beings, so when you give birth to them, they are forever; they are not just souls bound to earth, but they are eternal beings". I must honestly admit that I had never looked at it that way. I'm sure we can all say at times that we have a tendency to look at things from a very carnal and temporal perspective. While I opted to focus on the physical difficulties I would probably face again with pregnancy, she encouraged me to embrace both the earthly and spiritual perspective. This is why abortion is such a tragedy and child sacrificing is simply abhorrent. Infants and children are eternal beings regardless of when they are conceived and although one may opt to end a child's existence on planet earth, they are alive with God forever!

    I mentioned this to show how easily misinformed and distracted we can become with who we are in the natural. Abba not only made you, but He has also planned out your days. It is a brutal reality to know that we only have a fixed amount of days upon the earth and what we do with those days determines how we will live eternally. God told the Israelites in Jeremiah 29:11 that after they returned from Babylonian captivity, that He would revisit them and perform His good word toward them because He had good plans for them. His plans were plans of peace and not of evil, to give them a future and a hope but the people would have to determine if they actually wanted to experience the good plans God had for them. The Bible also says in Ecclesiastes 3:11 that God has planted eternity in our hearts, but even so, "people cannot see the whole scope of God's work from beginning to end" (NLT). The Lord has always had a plan for man, but it is the responsibility of man to draw close to Him in order to discover that plan. This is not a difficult thing. When your love and affection is for a particular person, you make time for them. You spend time with them. Their desires are your desires. You want to know what makes them happy and what makes them sad. You want to know what they like and dislike. If you truly love God, you will desire to know and follow Him. Jesus said in John 14:15, "If you love Me, keep My commandments." Part of becoming who you are in Christ is loving and following Him and this comes through relationship and communion with Him. This happens daily. The more time you spend with Him, the more you know about Him. The more you know about Him, the more He reveals who you are to Him.

Now let's discuss what it means to be made in the Father's image. Genesis 1:26 reads, "Then God said, 'Let Us make man in Our image, according to Our likeness; let them have dominion over the fish of the sea, over the birds of the air, and over the cattle, over all the earth and over every creeping thing that creeps on the earth.'" The Holy Godhead had a conversation and discussed their plan for man. The plan was to make man in "Our image" and according to "Our likeness."

The word "image" according to the Blueletter Bible lexicon is the Hebrew word "tselem" (masculine noun) which means "resemblance; a representative figure." It's like a statute created in the image of someone else. "Likeness" is the Hebrew word "demuwth" (adverb, feminine noun) that means "similitude, model, resemblance." Likeness has a lot to do with what we possess that is like the Holy Godhead. Some of the ways we are in the image of God are:

1. We are spirit beings. God is a Spirit according to John 4:24.
2. We can communicate with our God and He communicates with us (mostly spirit to Spirit). We have communicating faculties that allow us to have a loving relationship with Him.

3. We have physical faculties; we see, touch, hear, have hands, etc.

Some ways we are made in God's likeness are that:
4. We have knowledge and the ability to reason.
5. We have free choice.
6. We have intuition and imaginations (animals do not have).
7. We can love and have compassion.
8. We have certain creative abilities.

    Just as the Godhead of Heaven consists of three (3) distinct personalities; Father, Son and Spirit, so we have three (3) essential distinctions. Man is spirit, has a soul, and lives in a body according to 1 Thessalonians 5:23. Our physical bodies or flesh as we call it, make us world-conscious (hot, cold, etc.), our soul makes us self-conscious (mind, will, emotions) and our spirit makes us God-conscious. Our soul is connected to both the spiritual world and the natural world, and must decide if it will obey Holy Spirit and be in unity with God or obey the body/flesh, along with all of its temptations and worldly cravings. The soul has to decide who will be its master. At the fall of man, man's soul became slave to his flesh, but now that Jesus has redeemed us, your soulish man (at salvation) comes under the authority of your spirit man….the real you. When a believer has not subjected his/her soul to the rule of his/her spirit, he/she is what the Bible calls carnal (1 Corinthians 3:1,3).

    The Lord's desire, above all else, is for His creation to have a loving, thriving relationship with Him. Abba is not looking for our good works, although He appreciates them, but good works will never supersede love. He wants your heart. He wants you to get to know Him, to know His thoughts, to know His heart on any given matter. Our God is a loving Father who wants to give good gifts to His children (Matthew 7:11). Earthly fathers love their children, so why would our God be any different? As a matter of fact, His love is a perfect love. Our love is superficial at best and as much as we think we love our children, God loves us and them MORE!

    The more you become one with Jesus, the more you look and become like Him. The more you know His word, the more you sound like Him. The more infused you become with His Spirit, the more transformed you become. Abiding in Jesus deals with oneness and there can be no oneness without intimacy. Abide is the Greek word "meno" and it means "to continue to be present; not to depart; to remain as one" (Greek Lexicon). In John 15:4a, Jesus said, "Abide in me and I in you." This means that you are to continue to be present with Him: all of the time, all day, every hour. You should always anticipate His voice. You are to be attentive to the leading of the Holy Spirit. Dr. Francis Myles teaches in his book, The Consciousness of Now that, "We are to live every moment consciously aware of God's presence. We are not supposed to chase the future by forfeiting the present. When we live in the present and be present with the Lord, we encounter amazing things." Wow! How many people are always looking for tomorrow or for some big thing to happen in the future? Do you realize that when you do this, you are missing what God wants to do through you NOW?! I have come to realize that I miss out on so much precious time with God by looking to the future. My suggestion to you is …..enjoy today! Enjoy the moment you're presently in! Stop to hear what Holy Spirit is speaking to your heart. Take a look around you. Stop and see what God is doing NOW!

    So by now you should understand who created you but here's another astounding reality David captured in Psalm 8:4-6 when he said, "What is man that You are mindful of him And the son of man that You visit him? For You made him a little lower than the angels, And you crowned him with glory and honor. You have made him to have dominion over the works of Your hands; You have put all things under his feet." Did you read that? Your loving Father created you a little lower than Himself and crowned you with glory and honor. This is the reason why satan absolutely hates mankind. You carry God's glory! You remind him of God and the position he lost with God. Lucifer….now satan, was once arrayed in beauty and glory (Ezekiel 28:12) but his beauty was defiled and his glory departed due to pride, and now you wear the mantle of God's glory and are a constant reminder of what he lost! Your beauty is not an external beauty although God gives that to you as well. This God-given beauty begins in the heart and radiates outward.

      Your external behavior and thoughts are a reflection of the internal; your heart. Parents, you must be extremely careful with how you shape your child's beginning. From the womb, you should speak positive things over your child(ren) and read the Word to them while they are in the womb. Mothers, put headphones over your tummies and play worship music to your unborn babies. Don't allow your negative thoughts or events to cause you to see your children as anything less than blessed and favored. Whether you know it or not, your thoughts can be felt and/or discerned by your unborn child. You may have gotten pregnant unexpectedly and although you cannot change your current situation, you do have the opportunity to shape your child's future. Speak the Word of life over your children every day and ask Abba to let your eyes see them as He sees them. David said that we have dominion over the works of God's hands and have been given charge over everything created by God. You shape your world and your children's world by what you say and think (one of God's qualities), so guard your heart and guard your thoughts. This is Kingdom ruler-ship and will be discussed in a later chapter.

So, you have been fearfully and wonderfully made in the image of Christ. Nothing about you is a secret to God. You are an awesome wonder created by an awesome Creator. Don't allow anyone to tell you anything different. Don't let words of negativity prevent you from walking in the knowledge of your true Kingdom identity. Self esteem issues only triumph when people don't know who they are and don't have a sense of self-worth or understand their spiritual identity. My life has been radically changed now that I see myself as Jesus sees me. I no longer compare myself to others or think of myself as inferior to no one. There is a confidence I now embrace because my perspective has been changed. When I sing now, I understand that no one can sing like me because God created only one me. I don't have to try to sing like anyone else because I'm not them. There's a profound freedom that you can walk in once you embrace the uniqueness of your Heavenly identity. You are beautiful, you are loved and you belong to God!

CHAPTER TWO

DNA and Your Royal Bloodline

"And if you are Christ's, then you are Abraham's seed, and heirs according to the promise."
Galatians 3:29

As a human being, you have an earth suit called flesh; therefore, you are born through a bloodline. Your bloodline is your line of descent. Your bloodline has everything to do with your maternal and paternal descendants. Your bloodline encompasses your heritage, your ancestors, or your pedigree. DNA by definition is a molecule that contains the "instructions providing all of the information necessary for a living organism to grow and live inside the nucleus of every cell. These instructions tell the cell what role it will play in your body. DNA encodes a detailed set of plans, like a blueprint, for building different parts of the cell," (learn.genetics.utah.edu/content/molecules/dna/). These instructions are found inside every cell and are passed down from parents to their children. Each parent passes half of their chromosomes to each of their children.

The instructions written in your DNA determine how tall you will be, the color of your eyes, the melatonin in your skin, the texture of your hair, the size of your feet, your height, and other traits. Instructions are written and wrapped around like a spool or ladder and called a "helix." The letters mentioned above form words and these words make sentences. From my research findings, DNA is also called the "book of life." David understood in Psalm 139:14 that he had been awesomely (fearfully) and wonderfully made!

We live in a very complex world that promotes self-consciousness which makes it very difficult for Christians to walk in God-consciousness. For example, television is so inundated with self-idolization, materialism, power, fame, and pornography on every level that no wonder our children are perplexed about who they are. We are truly suffering from an identity crisis due to wrong external worldly ideologies and perspectives. Although the world has presented perverted philosophies of love, happiness and beauty, we as believers in the Lord Jesus Christ cannot allow the world to shape our views and beliefs regarding our self-worth and cause us to live to a different standard other than the one set by God.

To understand the blueprint of who you are, you must ask the Creator Himself. Now I know that may sound easier than actually doing it, but the Father is waiting to reveal to you who you are if you will just ask. Your God is intelligent beyond human words, and He has wondrously encrypted DNA within every human body that He designed to fulfill His purpose. He didn't miss a thing. Problems like low self-esteem only arise when a person cannot understand his or her value or worth from God's perspective. When you attempt to compare yourself to others or to the world, you will never measure up. Ah! But Jesus never compares you to anyone else and neither does He ask you to compare yourself with others. He made you uniquely different and celebrates your individuality. You should do the same.

Further, Dr. Myles' book on the DNA states that "God has His instructions concerning the fulfillment of His eternal purposes written in our DNA. Because of original sin in the garden, death agencies were introduced into man's bloodline and genetic makeup (you shall surely die). These death agencies (physical, spiritual and mentally) have caused a demonic genetic mutation. A mutation is when a gene or genetic sequence changes from its original or intended purpose. It can be caused by a variety of internal or external sources and the side effects can be positive or negative."

When you accepted Jesus as your Lord and Savior and Holy Spirit came to dwell within your heart, the process of metamorphosis began and your spirit man started the regeneration process. Romans 12:2 tells us not to be conformed to this world but to be transformed (changed/"metamorphoo") by the renewing of your minds. It is the amazing grace of your Lord Jesus that gives you the strength to overcome the power of sin by faith in the work of the cross. It is not your own works or abilities that obtain salvation. Your acceptance of Christ allows the Father to breathe His life into you so that your spirit man is awakened to the things of God's Kingdom. Your spirit man is no longer dormant and alienated from God. It is no longer ruled and governed by your un-generated soulish nature. Flesh man has been dethroned and spirit man takes the place of authority. While in the Garden of Eden, Adam was in God. When I say "in God," I am referring to the divine intimacy and oneness they shared. Adam had the mind of God and could therefore name all of the animals. His thoughts were in agreement with God's thoughts. No seed of corruption could be found in him before the fall. Adam walked in complete oneness with God, but when sin entered his DNA, he lost that divine fellowship with his Creator.

While I am certainly no expert in teaching DNA, I do find what I have read about the subject to be quite fascinating. For example, I am constantly finding new nuggets of truth unfolding. For instance, David said in Psalm 139:16, "Your eyes saw my substance, being yet unformed And in Your book they all were written, The days fashioned for me, When as yet there were none of them." For many years I have read this scripture and must admit that I was quite remiss in my reading. I looked at "Your book" simply as Heaven's book of life that has all of the names of God's chosen ones written in it (Revelation 3:5). The more I read Psalm 139 and studied the design and functionality of DNA, I became convinced that David, thousands of years ago, had great insight about DNA and he revealed to us this reality. This also confirmed for me how our cultures and mindsets can create great chasms in our ability to understand biblical times, etymology and middle eastern cultures if we are not led by Holy Spirit. Let's look further.

"DNA is an abbreviation for deoxyribonucleic acid. DNA is made up of four chemicals—adenine, guanine, cytosine and thymine—which are represented by the letters A, G, C and T. (http://lifehopeandtruth.com/god/is-there-a-god/intelligent-design/dna/). "In organisms called eukaryotes, DNA is found inside a special area of the cell called the nucleus. Because the cell is very small, and because organisms have many DNA molecules per cell, each DNA molecule must be tightly packaged. This packaged form of the DNA is called a chromosome. An organism's complete set of nuclear DNA is called its genome. The complete DNA instruction book, or genome, for a human contains about 3 billion bases and about 20,000 genes on 23 pairs of chromosomes," (https://www.genome.gov/25520880).

In Psalm 139:16, David stated that God's eyes saw him before he became a material being. The all-seeing eyes of God saw David's immaterial form first. God knew what He wanted David to look like and whom He desired for him to become. He would come through Jesse's line. He would be a mighty man of valor who would become king and rule God's people. Did David know this initially? No, but God knew who David would become and made sure that David's life unfolded according to His plan. In 1 Samuel 16 the Lord spoke to Samuel and sent him to Jesse's house because He had already selected Israel's next king. David was not even in the correct birth order among his brothers to become king, but God's ways always prevail. Verse 10 says that Jesse made seven (7) of his sons pass before Samuel but not one of them was God's chosen. David was the youngest of Jesse's sons, yet he was chosen for greatness. You may be feeling inadequate or unworthy or that you're not the correct person for the job, but like David, there's a great call for you. David was part of a royal bloodline and didn't even know it.

Have you ever thought about why you are not excelling at this point in your life? Could it be that you have not come into full realization of who you are and whose you are? There's royalty inside of you and the Father is waiting for you to embrace this truth. David's father and brothers saw him as a ruddy shepherd boy, but God saw him as the king of Israel! David's father and brothers saw him as he currently was, but God identified David according to his true identity even before his birth. Before you were conceived, God knew you, devised an awesome plan for your life, and wrote success in your DNA. Ask Jesus to give you an accurate perception of your true identity. Refuse to allow fear, anxiety, and lack of faith to rule you. Decide today to step into the divine blueprint that God has prepared for you.

The word substance, according to the Blue Letter online Interlinear word study, is the Hebrew word golem and it means, "fetus or embryo; the parts of which are not yet unfolded and developed." The word book is the Hebrew word cepher and it means, "instruction; written order; a kind of writing (written on a scroll)." So we can clearly see that the divine wisdom of the Father constructed David's form by writing it, or writing the instructions in/on a scroll. David said all his members were written. The word written is the Hebrew word kathab and it means, "to describe in writing; to write; record; to register; to continue writing; to decree; information that prescribes or directs." This means that all of his members or the various parts of his body were prescribed or described and written within a scroll. The word in continuance is the Hebrew word yowm which means "a division of time; period; days; lifetime" which means that instructions were written for the body to develop over a period of time. And finally the word fashioned is derived from the Hebrew word yatsar and it means "to be predetermined; to be formed (of human or divine activity); pre-ordain." So if we look at Psalm 139:16 according to the Hebrew definitions, we can clearly see that David understood the scroll or book to be a set of instructions written within his DNA for a specific period of time and this was all predetermined and written by an incredible God.

    Oh how magnificent it is to know that you and I have everything within us to achieve every God-given assignment! Your ability to learn, achieve, and succeed is already within your loins. Here's how I became awakened to this startling revelation. About a year and a half ago, my worship team and I attended a glory meeting just outside of Charlotte, North Carolina. I have been singing since I was a little girl but merely played around with trying to learn to play an instrument. During our prayer that night, the host of the glory meeting was praying for me, and one of the things she said was that not only would I sing but I would also play. Now I must be honest; I immediately went into a whirlwind of disbelief and developed what I call the "Sarah Syndrome" of unbelief for a brief moment because I had failed miserably at attempting to play the piano in years past. Nevertheless, the prophetic words resonated loudly within my spirit and I scribed the words in my prayer journal and tucked them away in my heart. A little time went by and every now and then that word would come back to me. I found myself constantly thinking about what instrument I would even attempt to try to play. Finally I concluded that since I loved the sound of the acoustic guitar, I would attempt to teach myself to play it; so off I went to Guitar Center and purchased my very first Epiphone acoustic guitar. Since I have two female guitarists on my worship team, I began to glean heavily from them. These wonderful young ladies would selflessly share simple guitar tricks and basic guitar chords information, and before long, I was putting chords and putting songs together.

To add to the previous prophetic word given to me, which was quickly becoming a reality, a few months later during a prophetic training session, I was given the exact same word by a totally different person. One of the ladies in the group told me that the Lord said not only would I sing, but I would also play; there was an instrument involved. So according to the scriptures, two witnesses had confirmed His Word for me and I knew this was something the Lord desired to make a reality in my life. As time went on, I rapidly grew in my ability to play the guitar and even wrote my first song and as time progresses, this is truly becoming a passion.

So why am I sharing this? I realized that although I was not aware of my ability to play an instrument, God knew I would play and sent word to me of His plan. He was letting me know that the ability or raw talent as we say, was already there and simply needed cultivating. So what does this mean for you? Encoded in your DNA are abilities and talents that you may not be aware of. Once the Lord "puts a demand" or reveals your hidden gift, don't exhaust yourself mentally trying to figure out how you're going to do it. The ability is there, so just pray and ask Holy Spirit to teach you. Utilize the resources around you and get to work. Whatever your call or ability or talent is, you must become vested in seeing its fulfillment. If it is not developed, it is your responsibility to start the process. Once I began to grasp the reality that I really could play the guitar and could actually play songs, my faith mounted to a whole new level. By faith, I would sit down and practice and trust Holy Spirit to allow me to tap into my inner abilities. If there's greatness inside of you, and there is, you must have the faith to step into it and trust in the Spirit of the Lord to help you bring it into full manifestation.

In Jeremiah 1:5, the Lord told Jeremiah that before He formed him in the womb, He knew him. "Knew" is the Hebrew word yada and means "to perceive and see, to know by experience or acquaintance." Before your mother and father ever met, God knew you and was acquainted with you. Before you came forth from the womb, God had already completed a great plan and tailor made it for your life! God's plan has already been written for your life, so now you must work your plan. He loves you and wants nothing but the best for you. He wants your will to align with His will. John 4:34 in the Complete Jewish Bible says, "Yeshua said to them, 'My food is to do what the one who sent me wants and to bring his work to completion.'" Jesus was strategically focused on doing the work of the Father and seeing the work through to its completion. This must be your plight also. You must endeavor to become all of what and who God has intended for you to become and remain vigilant in your pursuit of seeing His work to completion.

Now, let's talk about bloodline. Ever wonder why blood and bloodlines are so important to God? Leviticus 17:11 says, "For the life of the flesh is in the blood, and I have given it to you upon the altar to make atonement for your souls; for it is the blood that makes atonement for the soul," (emphasis mine). In this passage, scripture makes it clear that we, being flesh, are not to eat blood or anything that contains blood. The very thing that keeps us alive is the warm blood running through our veins. If you stop the flow of blood, man will cease to exist. The body, along with its cells and organs, is nourished and cleansed by blood. Life is in the blood. Genesis 4:10 says the voice of Abel's blood cried out from the ground. Contrary to what we see in the natural, when someone is murdered, it is his/her blood that cries out for justice before God in the realm of the spirit. Hebrews 12:24 says the blood of Jesus speaks (in the present) better things than the blood of Abel. When God breathed into man the breath of life, man received not only the breath of God, but also blood that would give and sustain his life. Blood is the seat of life and without it we cease to exist. The only remedy for the shedding of innocent blood is atonement through the sacrificing of blood. Blood defiles the land because it is life, God's life, that's in the blood and he demands justice for the innocent.

Looking further into this verse, it goes on to say that blood was to be used upon the altar to make atonement for your soul, which explains why the fig leaves that Adam and Eve sewed together for themselves were not sufficient. The fig leaves were made from trees; therefore, the efforts of their hands (works) only served to cover them instead of atonement. According to the Lord, sin must be atoned for, not covered. This is also why it is important to accept Jesus Christ as Lord and Savior and believe in His work on the cross because GOD REQUIRES ATONEMENT BY BLOOD, NOT COVERING!

There is power in the blood of Jesus and the most important thing the blood does is it redeems and atones! Man in all of his efforts has relentlessly attempted to attain salvation through his own efforts but has failed miserably. The Old Testament times dealt more with obeying laws and performing rites as a means of salvation and righteousness. The High Priest offered sacrifices on behalf of himself and the people for the atonement of sin once a year and this ceremonial sacrament had to be repeated every year. It was the blood of animals (i.e., goat, lamb, etc.) that served as substitution offerings for payment of mankind's sin. However, in the New Testament times, it was

Jesus, the Son and Lamb of God, who became man's true substitution offering for sin by shedding His blood on the cross (Galatians 4:4-5). We have been redeemed by the perfect Lamb of God. When you give your life and heart to Jesus, your slate is wiped clean. The blood of Christ stood in the gap for you and allowed God's judgment to rest upon Him. God judged man through Christ and now you are the redeemed of God!

Psalm 51:5 says, "Behold, I was brought forth in iniquity, And in sin my mother conceived me." This verse clearly states that we are brought forth in iniquity and conceived in sin. There was nothing we did specifically to be born into sin; iniquity and sin already existed in the bloodline and DNA of humanity. We were all born guilty of the original sin brought forth by Adam and Eve because we, too, are born of flesh and blood. Eve was/is the mother of all humans, and all human beings came through Eve and Adam. The guilt of man's original sin against God is what passed through the bloodline from generation to generation until Jesus. In every family, there are certain things or traits that are passed on through your bloodline by those who preceded you. These things can be bad or good; however, you had no control of preventing them from entering your bloodline. Later on in this chapter, I will briefly explain what you can do to renounce evil or bad things that have entered your family's bloodline.

But here's the wonderful news. The Father had a plan from the very beginning regarding your redemption! Following the downfall of man, God initiated His plan of salvation from the penalty of eternal judgment. When man disobeyed God's direct order and took of the forbidden tree, there were several deaths pronounced upon humanity. Man became partaker of eternal judgment (eternal and spiritual); man then became subject to physical death and his body began the decaying process; and man (his soul, that is) would also die emotionally in that he would be alienated from God and no longer enjoy intimate fellowship with his Creator on a moment-by-moment basis. Lastly, man would die morally. Man's ability to follow God wholeheartedly had been tainted and perverted by satan, and man was forced to live by the dictates of his lustful, wayward heart.

So let's look at God's solution to man's depravity. Genesis 3:15 says, "And I will put enmity Between you and the woman, And between your seed and her Seed; He shall bruise your head, and you shall bruise His heel." God said that there would be hatred between the woman's seed (Christ) and the serpent (satan). The Father set a prophetic decree in motion by declaring that the Seed of the woman would bruise the head of the serpent and the serpent would bruise the heel of Jesus. The cross was where the serpent bruised the heel of Jesus, causing his death to come at the hands of man, but the cross was also the first stage of the devil's defeat, or the bruising of his head. Jesus came as flesh, i.e., a man, in order to bear our judgment in his body. Through the blood of Jesus, God could judge humanity without destroying the entire human race!

Paul said in 1 Corinthians 1:18 that the cross is foolishness to those who are perishing but to us who are being saved, it is the power of God. Hallelujah! When you come to accept Jesus as your Lord and Savior, you are born again, meaning you have a new bloodline! Your bloodline is no longer tainted with the stain of sin and judgment. You are no longer held bondage by the sins of your mothers and fathers and ancestors. At salvation, you are transferred into the pure and perfect bloodline of Jesus Christ and though your sins be as scarlet, Jesus washes them white as snow (Isaiah 1:18). 2 Corinthians 5:21 says, "For He made Him who knew no sin to be sin for us, that we might become the righteousness of God in Him." Jesus was completely sinless and made to be a sin offering on your behalf, and your union with Him is what makes you righteous before God. Jesus did it all and Jesus paid it all. The only thing you have to do is believe in the power of the blood and receive His righteousness. It is not by man's good works or man's righteousness that he obtains right standing with God but only through the precious blood of the Lamb.

      God requires blood for atonement. The judgment upon man required a blood sacrifice. The law demanded judgment and the judgment had to be paid. In any legal system, judgments must be satisfied. Most people don't realize that the Kingdom of God is a legal system. There are spiritual laws that govern God's Kingdom and violations of these laws result in consequences and penalties. The blood was a legal transaction. Instead of Abel's blood and the blood of others that cry out for vengeance, Hebrews 12:24 says that Jesus mediates the new covenant between God and man in that His blood speaks of forgiveness. Abel's blood cries out for justice but Jesus' blood cries out for forgiveness. The pure, undefiled blood of Jesus was offered on the cross of Calvary and was also sprinkled on the mercy seat of Heaven, thereby making us right with God and giving us access to God. By means of death, He redeemed your transgressions under the old covenant (Hebrews 9:15). You are now adopted and bear the name of your Father. This is why the devil hates for us to talk and sing about the blood! There is power in the blood of Jesus! Salvation and healing came through the pure blood of Jesus! Justice was satisfied because of the blood of Jesus. You have been made righteous (put in right standing with God) only because of the blood of Jesus! No one else's blood can save you and declare you righteous except the blood of our Lord and Savior Jesus Christ! Jesus not only died for you; He became you so that your sins would be eradicated. You are victorious only through His precious blood.

Dr. Francis Myles currently hosts amazing conferences worldwide called "Jumping the Bloodline." It is one of the most life-changing conferences I have ever attended. Dr. Myles says, "Jumping the Line is simply a powerful prophetic act of faith that symbolizes the fact that you are crossing over any kind of hindrance through the power of the Cross; whether those hindrances are generational curses, bad habits, wrong genetic dispositions, physical ailments, financial hardships, addictions or oppressions." This conference was birthed after the release of his book Breaking Generational Curses Under the Order of Melchizadek. There is so much I could say about this topic but I am living proof that if we fail to repent for specific sins, iniquities and/or transgressions, we could be limiting our ability to walk in the fullness of what Christ obtained for us. When we renounce sins passed on through our maternal and paternal bloodlines and take on the pure and perfect bloodline of Jesus Christ, those things that were written in our DNA because of sin, no longer have dominion over us or our children. You have the power to stop generational curses right now! Don't think for one minute that sins and iniquities cannot be passed on. All of us can take a quick look down our family's history and identify behaviors, sicknesses, disorders, and other dysfunctions that have constantly repeated themselves in our families. You can put a stop to it now through the finished work of the cross because you are part of a pure and perfect bloodline.

Not only does the blood deliver you from past judgment, but the work of salvation is steadily working in you at the present, keeping you from the power and grips of sin. It will also be the atoning work of Jesus that will remove sin from your life today and His grace will give you the ability to live right before Him. You see, the blood and cross have a past, present and future work. When you confess and repent of your wrongdoings, Jesus stands before the Father on your behalf, and the Father no longer sees your faults but rather, He sees Jesus and His blood sacrifice. When the accuser of the brethren accuses you before the Father, your confession and repentance allows the blood of Jesus to continually answer for you.

What am I saying in this chapter? Jesus has settled the score for you. He has made the wrongs right. He has made you a friend of God. The undefiled blood of Jesus satisfied the judgment in Heaven against humanity. You no longer have to live as a slave under the bondage of sin. Holy Spirit will help you live a life free of sin's grip. Your bloodline can be cleansed and as long as you remain humble before the Lord and confess and repent of current shortcomings because there is no condemnation that can keep you from entering God's presence! You are now a descendant of a royal bloodline. When you accepted Jesus, you took on royalty and His bloodline is now your bloodline. You have a new identity. You are a citizen of Heaven with Heavenly authority. You are now in a legal position to be identified with Christ. To adopt means to take as one's own and that's what Christ did for you. You have been legally adopted as a son of God (son has nothing to do with gender) and because you are a son, you are an heir. This is the greatest truth the enemy would love to hide from God's people. It is extremely crucial that you begin to see yourself as a son of God and change the way you've seen yourself in the past. You have authority, you have dominion, you have purpose and you have a rich heritage in Jesus Christ!

Veronica Evans

THE IMPORTANCE OF REPENTANCE

Let me speak very briefly about the topic of repentance because it has become almost obsolete in the church today. It is an astounding reality to know that regardless of what I do wrong, there is no sin greater than God's ability to heal and forgive me. When I do wrong, I have an advocate, Jesus, who intercedes for me. But here's the fallacy I see today. There are many who teach that because grace covers past, present and future sins, there's no need to repent. Deception! Deception! Deception! The enemy wants you to adopt this heresy. 1 John 1:9 says, "If we confess our sins, He is faithful and just to forgive us our sins and to cleanse us from all unrighteousness." John is talking to New Testament believers, not unbelievers. James 5:16 even tells us to confess our trespasses to one another, pray for one another, that you may be healed. Failure to confess and repent gives the adversary a right to accuse you before God. I personally believe that some Christians suffer various oppressions and sicknesses because of failure to confess and repent of wrongdoings.

But once again, here's the good news. Jesus stands ready to forgive! It is not a bad thing; it's a wise thing to repent. Repent of anything you have failed to confess, even if it was done prior to your salvation days. There are doors we open up to the enemy that we can close through repentance and faith. Renounce habits, sicknesses and/or sinful acts you see in your family bloodlines. Repent for the acts of your former ancestors and receive the pure bloodline of Jesus. Remember that I mentioned how things can be passed on through your bloodline that your mother, father, maternal or paternal family members could have committed. An example could be a family who had a great grandmother who participated in witchcraft. Although you did not personally commit the sin, ask the Father for forgiveness on behalf of your great grandmother so that the sin of witchcraft does not continue to pass through your bloodline. If you're like me, you can probably identify certain behaviors, sicknesses, etc. within your family that have passed from one generation to another, but if you can identify the root or origin, lift that up before Jesus through confession and repentance, and you be the one to stop the behavior or sickness from passing on to another generation.

For those who may think this is nonsense, I am a living witness for what I am saying. Here's something very personal I would like to share. There was something I had done before I became saved that was manifested after I became a Christian. It was not until Holy Spirit spoke to a very special friend of mine and told me that I needed to curse this past sin at the root. The word my friend gave me came from Galatians 6:7-8, "Be not deceived, God is not mocked; for whatever a man sows, that he will also reap. For he who sows to his flesh will of the flesh reap corruption, but he who sows to the Spirit will of the Spirit reap everlasting life." Initially, I was a bit bewildered because I thought that once I became a Christian EVERY sin in my past was done away with and could never brought up again. Well, let's just say that I did not fully understand the Word. It was not until I confessed my wrongdoing specifically and cursed that sin at the root, that I was no longer tormented because of it and reaping its consequences. When I say "curse at the root", I am referring to going back in your mind to where the sin originally took place, confess your wrongdoing, and ask the Father for forgiveness. Please hear me on this. I am not saying that everything wrong or bad is tied to a specific sin, but when things are happening in your life contrary to the promises of God, try to trace things back to their root to see if a wrong door was opened to the enemy and deal with it from there.

In order to walk in your kingdom identity, you must openly confess transgressions, iniquities or sins and repent because what you do to and through your body has physical and spiritual repercussions. Subsequently, the quickest way to deal with shortcomings is confession and repentance. Think of it this way: you will never kill a tree unless you kill the roots. The tree that needs "killing" is sin, but you must kill it with humility, faith, confession and repentance. So what if it takes a few more minutes in prayer. At least you can walk away feeling the liberty and peace of God versus judgment, uncertainty, and self-condemnation.

Your DNA has been interwoven with that of Jesus Christ's blood. You are now part of the royal family of God. His blood is now your life source. He exchanged His life for yours. You have a divine code written within you with a purpose ready to be accomplished. The blood now gives you access to the presence of God. You have been engrafted into the pure and royal bloodline of Jesus Christ and you represent Him in the earth. When the enemy sees you, he sees the blood! Embrace the power of the cross today. You are a new creation with a new Father and new brethren. You are a child of the King and a citizen of Heaven. You can live in this profound reality daily and change your world. Remove the garments of self-doubt, failure, worldly stereotypes, sickness, heaviness, timidity, and put on the royal garments of love, joy, peace, righteousness, praise, authority, and wisdom. You are regal and you are royal!

CHAPTER THREE

Come Out of Her

"Then I heard another voice out of heaven say: 'My people, come out of her! so that you will not share in her sins, so that you will not be infected by her plagues, for her sins are a sticky mass piled up to heaven, and God has remembered her crimes.'"
Revelation 18:4-5 (CJB)

    I love the book of Revelation; as a matter of fact, it is my favorite book of the Bible. Because of its prophetic nature and plethora of symbolism, I am very careful in my approach to this very profound book. Seeing through the eyes of the Spirit is key to understanding the book of Revelation and the entire Bible. There is an implicit warning at the end of the book of Revelation for those who would attempt to change or water down the words of this prophetic letter. Revelation 22:18-19 says, "I warn everyone hearing the words of the prophecy in this book that if anyone adds to them, God will add to him the plagues written in this book. And if anyone takes anything away from the words in the book of this prophecy, God will take away his share in the Tree of Life and the holy city, as described in this book," (CJB).

    I am a worship leader and the book of Revelation helped me understand the power of worship for the believer. I have led worship in the local church setting for over twenty years. Several years ago, the Lord led me to put together a worship team of minstrels and psalmists to lead worship both outside and inside the local church. Worship is my life. It is who I am. It is also what I do. I love ministering to the Lord and allowing Him to minister back to me. I love being swept off my feet by my bridegroom and carried away into holy bliss. Sound strange? Then you really haven't worshipped yet!

David found the path to the secret place of the Father. He found the path to the Heavenly Jerusalem (Hebrews 12:22, "But you have come to Mount Zion and to the city of the living God, the heavenly Jerusalem, to an innumerable company of angels") and that my friends is what I have found also.

When meditating, researching, and praying about the topic of identity and what it means to operate in the Kingdom, the first thing that came to mind involved discovering and honing in on the various hindrances that can prevent one from walking in the fullness of Kingdom identity and authority. The verse of scripture that immediately came to mind was Revelation 18:4, which is scribed above.

This chapter is going to challenge you. It is going to cause your flesh man to resist if it is not already dead. It is going to go against the grain of what is being currently taught but is not biblical. Should your flesh be confronted and crucified on a regular basis? Absolutely! So let's get started.

In order to understand Revelation chapter 18, we must first take a glance at chapter 17. Chapter 17 deals with Babylon but not Babylon the city. Revelation 17:5 refers to Babylon as "Mystery Babylon The Great." During my time of research and study, I have come to know that there are two distinct references to Babylon in the book of Revelation and they are different. Revelation chapter 17 talks about mystery Babylon, i.e., the mother of harlots, and Revelation chapter 18 reveals the fall of Babylon the Great. For clarity, mystery Babylon (the harlot) deals with Babylon the religious system or the false religious church, and Babylon the Great deals with a political and economic system.

Throughout the remainder of this book I will also be discussing the different roles or functions you have been given in the Kingdom of God. Not only are you given various roles and functions but you are also expected to operate in these roles. Failure to function in your Kingdom role has so many hindrances and possible dangers to your spiritual growth. According to dictionary.com, the word function means "The kind of action or activity proper to a person, place or institution; the purpose for which something is designed or exist." God created Adam and Eve and His main desire was to create them for fellowship. They were to function as His agents in the earth and carry out His will. We, too, were created to have fellowship with God, and when satan sought to destroy that fellowship, Abba, Jesus and Holy Spirit immediately devised a plan to restore the broken fellowship. There is a certain level of authority you automatically receive when you decide to walk in your designated Kingdom inheritance but you must know and understand how to apply Kingdom strategies in order to carry out God's will for your life.

     Before we learn about how to walk in your Kingdom authority, let's continue to sanctify (set apart) ourselves. Paul said in 1 Corinthians 11:28 that before we take communion, we are to examine ourselves. The Greek word for examine is dokimazo and it means "to test, scrutinize, to see whether a thing is genuine or not, deem worthy." Therefore, in order to operate in the fullness of your Kingdom authority and inheritance, you must first acknowledge where you are in relation to your current walk with the Lord. You must be in a constant mode of examining your heart and weighing your actions. If they are contrary to the Lord's ways, then by grace you can change them. In John 15:18, Jesus tells His disciples that they are not of (belong to) the world, therefore the world would hate them. You have been called to function and think totally different from that of non-believers, so don't be surprised when the world rejects you. Jesus said to Pilate in John 18:36 in the Complete Jewish Bible that His kingship did not derive its authority from this world's order of things. The things of God's Kingdom are of a higher and different order than the Kingdoms of this world, and because you now understand this reality, you must live according to Heaven's Kingdom principles. You MUST make an identity change today and take on the life that comes from Jesus.

Babylon; the Culture

Let's talk about Babylon; the city, the culture, and why God commands His people in these last days to "come out of her." According to the Bible, Nimrod was the son of Cush and the great grandson of Noah (Genesis 10:8). Nimrod was the first powerful ruler of the earth whose heart was hostile towards God and was known for constructing the infamous tower of Babel, which is where we get the name Babylon. The words babel and Babylon mean confusion (by mixing). It was the place where God came down and saw how the people, under the leadership of Nimrod, were attempting to construct a city and tower that reached to Heaven in complete opposition of Him (Genesis 11). Josephus, a first century Romano-Jewish scholar and historian, said Nimrod "persuaded them not to ascribe it to God as if it was through his means they were happy, but to believe that it was their own courage which procured that happiness." Josephus also wrote that it was Nimrod who turned the hearts of the people away from God and changed the government into tyranny by causing the people to depend on his power instead of God's.

The Babylonian religion was founded by Nimrod's wife, Semiramis (who is believed to have also been his father's wife). Historical writings state that she was a high priestess of idol worship and that she gave birth to a son whom she claimed was conceived miraculously. The son's name was

Tammuz and he was considered to be a savior. Sound familiar? It was also said that Tammuz was killed by a wild beast and then miraculously brought back to life.

Tammuz is the "deity" that the Easter holiday is patterned after. Ishtar, also known as, Semmaramis and pronounced Easter, commemorated this day in reverence to their god Tammuz whom she deified, along with other gods believed to be different types of saviors. They believed Tammuz was the only begotten of the sun-goddess and the moon-goddess, (http://www.lasttrumpetministries.org/tracts/tract1.html). Tammuz was also believed to be fond of rabbits, which made them therefore sacred to this newly found religion. Again it was believed that Tammuz was the son of the sun-god Baal, whom some believed was really Nimrod reincarnate. So every year, the first Sunday after the full moon at the beginning of the spring equinox, Queen Semmaramis or Ishtar's Sunday, was celebrated with rabbits and eggs. See where I'm going? To enlighten you even further, Constantine the Great, a Roman emperor, convened the Council of Nicaea in 325 AD. This council unanimously ruled that the Easter festival should be celebrated throughout the Christian world on the first Sunday after the full moon following the vernal equinox; and if the full moon should occur on a Sunday and thereby coincide with the Passover festival, Easter should be commemorated on the Sunday following. So in the Christian communities, the pagan holiday of Easter is celebrated while Passover has been replaced, (http://www.babylonforsaken.com/easter.html).

I could go on and on telling you all about how Easter never was a Christian holiday. It has nothing to do with Jesus and His resurrection. Passover was the holiday celebrated by the early Christians and New

Testament believers as well. It commemorates the blood sacrifice by the slain Lamb of God for humanity and His glorious resurrection.

      The early morning sunrise services of Easter also tie into the early rising on the sun-day, the worship of Tammuz. In Ezekiel 8:13-17 God showed Ezekiel how His people worshipped idols in HIS house! Let me say that I am certainly not trying to ruin your holiday celebrations; however, I do feel it's important for you to know the origin of your traditions. It's next to impossible to embrace pagan celebrations and try to "Christianize" them and make them acceptable. My one objective here is to show you how some of the traditions, customs, and religious activities we celebrate have pagan roots of which most of us are totally unaware. The Lord challenged me several years ago to study the origins of the Easter and Christmas holidays. He told me to research them and find out the root of their existence. Because my kids were young at the time, I felt compelled to have annual Easter egg hunts, decorate Christmas trees, and participate in other holiday festivities. While I have never been a fan of jolly old Saint Nick and have always told my children that he did not exist, I still found myself participating in the Christmas and Easter holidays in some way without fully knowing their origin. I was challenged to change my perspective. I was challenged to remove my family and myself from the commercialization of them and completely change my focus. I do understand that this may not be your conviction. My point here is to simply reveal to you how there are things that we do out of habit and not with godly knowledge and understanding. So my suggestion to you is ask Holy Spirit what you should and should not celebrate. I have heard many nonbelievers scoff at Christians because they look worldlier than the world. Non-believers know that a lot of the Western holidays are pagan and don't understand why Christians still celebrate them. God gave us the feasts to observe for a specific reason. God fulfilled major bible prophecy during the feast times and He designed these feast times to be "set times" for the church. Are these feasts for the Jews only? No. Are we not the seed of Abraham according to Galatians 3:29. Please hear me when I say I'm not attempting to be legalistic here. As believers, I do believe we have the responsibility to know what does and does not glorify our Father.

Worship: the Foundation

I love the Father because He never wants His children to be clueless or ignorant. Jesus told the Samaritan woman at the well that she worshipped what she didn't know (John 4:22). The Samaritans set up a rival worship place on the top of Mount Gerizim and felt they were worshipping in the correct worship location and worshipping the correct God. Although they tried to make their location and their worship attitude authentic, its foundation was not laid upon the correct God. As a matter of fact, Jesus told the woman that salvation came through the Jews, yet the Samaritans were trying to circumvent the Jews and the Jewish religion. Still today there are tens of thousands of religions today but Jesus said that the only faith that God will accept is that which came through the Jews (The Wiersbe Bible Commentary). Can we change that? No! Can we create another way or another religion to circumvent what has already been established? No! Can we change the nationality of people the Lord decided to send the Messiah through? No!

Our God is holy and He will have nothing to do with any form of idolatry. It doesn't matter how we attempt to "Christianize" certain holidays, activities, locations, and so on. If the holiday is not grounded in scripture and in compliance with God's nature, we cannot expect Him to accept it. Our worship must be authentic and it must glorify Abba Father. Worship is the foundation for eliminating baals and false gods that have been set up in your life. Paul urges the church in 1 Corinthians 6:11-18 to be holy. He asked the Corinthian Church a series of questions on the subject of idol worship and holiness. One specific question was, "And what agreement has the temple of God with idols?" Paul went on to tell them that they were the temple of the living God and to "Come out from among them and be separate, says the Lord," (2 Corinthians 6:17). Paul was not telling the believers that they could not associate with unbelievers, but instead, they should not compromise and indulge in sinful practices. This is so key for us today. We cannot take on the mindset of the world and be drawn into its philosophical views of morality. There is a standard of righteousness and holiness that God has called you to, and He does not decrease or let down His standard. Worship will keep you in a posture of humility. When you reverence and honor the Lord daily, He will show you things and ways that are not in alignment with His will for you. As you shed yourself of these things, His light becomes brighter in you. His anointing will become evident upon you and you begin to carry the indelible glory of your Father.

Setting Yourself Apart Continually

To walk in your true identity means aligning yourself with Kingdom principles and standards. It means righteous living. It means putting away selfish ambitions. It means setting yourself apart for God and living the way the Bible instructs you to live. It means putting on the life of a Kingdom citizen and living your life for Jesus. It means loving beyond your human capability to love. Every believer must strive to maintain integrity before God and man.

Christ was the epitome of integrity and holiness. He let nothing and no one alter his thinking regarding who He was and the standard He was to uphold. You cannot let anything cause you to step out of alignment with God. This setting apart is continual. This setting apart must be intentional. It will require a counting up the cost and embracing the responsibility, but in spite of it all, it's going to be worth it! Our God is so awesome. What He desires to give you pales in comparison to any sacrifice you will ever make for Him. These sacrifices are miniscule compared the joy you will experience as you become one with Christ and the perpetual delight you will experience with Him in eternity. As you shed off your old self, put on Christ and all of His glory. His image will become your image. You will become like a chaste bride awaiting the arrival of her bridegroom. Can you hear the Lord saying, "Come away with Me?" That's His desire for you, to come away and be separated unto Him.

Religious Babylon

Revelation 17 deals with the antichrist and religious Babylon. Revelation 17:6 says, "I saw the woman drunk from blood of God's people, that is, from the blood of the people who testify about Yeshua," (CJB). The main thing I want to point out here is that in these last days, there will be a convergence of many different false religions that will seek to unite all religions into one religion and dominate the world. This false religion will intoxicate the masses. If you haven't heard it yet, the goal of many governments, including ours, is to move the world into a One World Religion controlled by one world leader; the New World Order as most of you have heard. This upcoming religious system seeks to merge all religions into one and will appear in the natural to be spiritual. It will be attractive and embraced by many because of its humanitarian undertones and inclusivity of all people regardless of religious belief, but in this new system, kings and nations will commit fornication with the great harlot Babylon. In the Bible, harlotry deals with infidelity. It is a turning away from someone or something you once solidly committed your faithfulness to. It is a turning away from God and the things of God and entertaining the ways of satan and the ways of the world. It is playing the prostitute. Leaders and nations, who once appeared to know and follow God, will turn their backs on God and intentionally mislead people. Though this system, the woman, will appear regal and great, she will be full of abominations and filthiness and unclean acts that will disgust our God. This new religious order will do abhorrent things and require that everyone else oblige.

In today's society there has grown an intense desensitization towards godly things. God's Word is being watered down in order to appease the masses, and morality has been totally thrown out the window. The "greasy" or "hyper" grace phenomenon has swept the church. While we are grateful to God for His amazingly, indescribable grace, we must be careful not to take His grace for granted or make it ineffective. Grace does NOT give Christians a license to sin! Paul said in Romans 6:1, "What shall we say then? Shall we continue in sin that grace may abound?" Then he answered his own question in verse 2 by declaring, "Certainly not!" He then said if we have died with Christ, meaning we are no longer ruled or governed by our flesh, then how can we continue to do something we have been freed from? I believe the enemy has enticed many believers to think it's okay to habitually sin because grace will cover it. I also believe he's led some leaders to teach that there's no need to confess and repent because grace covers your past, present and future sins. If this were true, James would not have said in 5:16 to "Confess your trespasses to one another, and pray for one another, that you may be healed." If there was no need to confess and repent, then John would not have said in 1 John 1:9, "If we confess our sins, He is faithful and just to forgive us our sins and to cleanse us from all unrighteousness." The word "if" means this is conditional. If means IF you confess your sins THEN God will be faithful to forgive you and cleanse you from all unrighteousness. If you never confess them, those transgressions are not forgiven and you give the enemy access to create strongholds in your life. Don't give the enemy a foothold. Repentance and confession are good and necessary for spiritual vitality and maturity.

      What am I saying? Stay alert! Study the Word of God consistently and pray all the time. The times are changing swiftly and you cannot afford to be caught off guard. Religious Babylon will deceive those who do not understand God's Word or His ways. Kingdom authority is given to those who have submitted themselves to the teaching of Holy Spirit. He is the Master Teacher and will teach you all things. He will tell you of things to come and how to respond to them. Prayer is your lifeline and the Word is your sword. And although religious Babylon will present herself as godly, Holy Spirit will allow you to see her deception and give you strategies for how to move forward in your purpose.

Illustration

I used to be borderline anemic, so I craved ice a lot. While I loved all types of ice, I really loved shaved ice. I would stand in the door of my freezer with a cup and scrape the ice into my cup, to the brim. As I ate the ice, there was such gratification to my taste buds because my body was clearly missing something vital. In my case, anemia was the result of an iron deficiency. From my research, I have discovered that doctors use the term "pica" to describe these craving for non-food related items that have no nutritional value whatsoever. Some people who are anemic even crave things like dirt, sand, starch, and baking soda. When I changed my diet and began to call on the name of the Lord for healing, something changed. When I visited my doctor for my annual wellness visit, all of my blood work came back normal. I know that God completely healed me from anemia, and the cravings for ice stopped. I have no desire to order cups of ice from the restaurant or stand in my freezer door and chisel away at the icebox. Why? The root of the problem has been taken care of and even if a person is sitting next to me eating ice, I am no longer tempted to join them. Why? Because the root cause of this deficiency had been eradicated.

This is what Christ did for you! When you accept Jesus as your Lord and Savior, the old nature within you changes; therefore, the behaviors that you once craved are methodically removed as long as you remain IN Him. This doesn't mean you won't mess up from time to time, but you're no longer driven or governed by your sinful nature because you are dying to your fleshly nature day by day, because the thing that once held you captive has been removed. You should no longer crave things that go against your new nature because Holy Spirit has taken up residence within you. Look at what Jude said in Jude 1:4 (NLT), "I say this because some ungodly people have wormed their way into your churches, saying that God's marvelous grace allows us to live immoral lives. The condemnation of such people was recorded long ago, for they have denied our only Master and Lord, Jesus Christ." Wow! There you have it. Jude said it was already predicted long ago that ungodly people would try to deceive the people of God regarding the topic of grace by telling them it's okay to live immoral lives (debauchery is a living life according to sensual pleasures); that God's grace would cover them. Need I say more about this false teaching on hyper or greasy grace? Jesus died so that sin would longer dominate you and me. He died so that you could live a life free from the bondage of sin and the fear of death. He conquered the stronghold of sin for you forever!

    I am really passionate about biblical truth and remaining separated for God because I have heard so many erroneous teachings that are leading God's people astray today. You are the bride of Christ and He's coming back for you. He's coming for a bride that has been set apart for Him with no divided affections. He's coming back for those who have remained undefiled and faithful and have not played the harlot with the world or the ways of the world. Sin is bondage and Jesus wants His people to live in total freedom. If you are struggling with any form of sin, transgression, or iniquity, Jesus is standing and waiting for you to run to Him for healing and deliverance. Once you have confessed and repented (turned away), that's all you need. Remember that repentance means turning away. It is not willful and habitual participation. By faith, receive the forgiveness of Jesus and Holy Spirit will give you the grace and power you need to keep that stronghold at bay.

Veronica Evans

Come Out of Her

Revelation 18 deals with Babylon the Great, which is the political, social, and economic (commercial) system. The Bible says that this Babylon has become a dwelling place of (for) demons and a prison for every unclean (foul) spirit and a cage of every unclean bird. The nations have drunk of the wine of the wrath of her fornication. The kings of the earth have committed fornication with her, and she has made rich the merchants of the earth through the abundance of her luxury (verses 2, 3). While we know in this chapter that judgment has been pronounced and this great city will be no more because the angel declares it has fallen, the part that really caught my attention was the beckoning to the BELIEVERS to "come out of her!"
Now if this city is as obviously corrupt as the Bible says it will be, how is it that believers of the Lord Jesus Christ will be intertwined with such evil? How can those who have tasted of the heavenly call be acquainted and indulged in such degradation? But wait! The revelator is talking about commercial and economic Babylon. He is talking about materialism, the desire for more, the riches of the world, the insatiable desire for status and power, the incomprehensible, never-ending yearning and wanting for more!

We live in a culture where there's no contentment for what we have. I look at how I grew up as a child and how my children are growing up today, and it seems like my children are never satisfied. My daughter has more toys than what you'll find in any store, yet every time we go into a store, her little heart is steadily looking to add to her already overflowing collection of stuff. Paul said in Philippians 4:11 that whatever state he found himself to be in, he had "learned" how to be content. Contentment is not something we are born with. Actually, it is the very opposite of our sinful nature. Paul had to teach himself how to be content. No matter how much his nature desired more, he had to practice being okay with what he had and where he was in life at the present time. Let me say this, if you cannot be happy and content in the present with what you have, you certainly won't appreciate your future. We must learn to embrace and enjoy the NOW in order to have a greater appreciation for what lies ahead.

Here is what I hear Holy Spirit saying right now, "Greed is the seed for discontentment!" When you set your eyes on continually gaining more, you rob yourself from the joy and satisfaction of what you have currently achieved. Babylon will be the place of enticement. It will use wealth, materialism, power and self-ambition as its bait. Once its hooks are set, people will become prey to the enemy and a recipient to the wrath set against the great city Babylon, which is symbolic of this world's system.

You cannot afford to mingle good and evil, leaven with unleaven, and light with darkness. Again, Paul admonished the Corinthian Church in 2 Corinthians 6:14-15 not to be unequally yoked with unbelievers. Then he asked them a question, "For what fellowship has righteousness with lawlessness? And what communion has light with darkness? And what accord has Christ with Belial? Or what part has a believer with an unbeliever?" Paul was saying you cannot mix good and evil. There is no middle ground between the two. It's either good or evil. I know this may seem a bit dissonant, but these are things I have learned throughout my journey with the Lord. You cannot mix the holy with the profane. When you participate in lying, sexual immorality, unforgiveness, gossiping, murmuring and complaining, murder, bitterness, and the like, you must understand that these are the works of flesh, and those who practice them will not inherit the Kingdom of God (Galatians 5:21). It is God's desire that no one is lost but that all should come to Him in repentance (2 Peter 3:9), but the choice is yours. Abba is holy and it is His Holy Spirit in us that helps us become holy as well.

I truly believe that we, the body of Christ, do not walk in the true authority and inheritance Jesus desires for us when we refuse to forsake the ways of Babylon. The ways of Babylon are contrary to the ways of God's Kingdom. Hebrews 12:14 says that without holiness, no one will see the Lord. My sincerest desire is to bring the people of God to the knowledge of the truth so they can live victorious lives through Christ. Jesus said in Matthew 7:13-14, "Enter through the narrow gate; for wide is the gate and broad is the way that leads to destruction, and there are many who go in by it. Because narrow is the gate and difficult is the way which leads to life, and there are few who find it." The way that Jesus provides is a costly way, and a lonely way BUT it leads to life! This is the way of love and it is also the way of transparency. The majority of the world will take the broad way. They will enjoy the appetites and glamour of the broad way but it will lead to utter ruin. Christianity is NOT a pie in the sky type of religion. It demands accountability and responsibility to one another and to our God. Jesus clearly said that the narrow way is difficult and He admonishes us to strive or press to enter through this right gate. The reality is this, you cannot travel two roads at the same time that are heading in two different directions. You must choose. Jesus has even told us the path to take, but the decision is still ultimately yours. Will you walk the path that's less convenient, less glamorous and popular, or will you sacrifice popularity now for Heavenly joy and fulfillment later?

Let me give you a real but difficult decision in my initial turning away from Babylon. All my life I have desired nothing more than to be a professional singer. I had dreams as a little girl that I would be a famous singer. I sang in beauty pageants during my school years and won trophies for my talent. I sang in the church choirs, won numerous talent shows, and made quite a name for myself. In 1992 I auditioned for Star Search and made the cut! I was the unknown young adult from a small town called Mount Olive, North Carolina, with nothing but a big dream that seemed to be lurking on the horizon. I won several of the competitions on Star Search and had the opportunity to actually meet the legendary Ed McMahon! My dark, alto tone voice along with the skill of poised stage presence landed me a spot in the semi-final and final rounds.

One interesting event happened tho. The night before the finals, I dreamt that I lost in the finals round. After sharing my dreamy with my husband, he lovingly tried to convince me that it was only a dream, regardless of how real I told him it was to me. Long story short, I lost the finals round that forked over a nice amount of prize money to a country singer. Although I'm not knocking country singers, I am knocking the fact that I had already won against this very same country singer in a previous round so I couldn't understand why things had reversed.

Nevertheless, my fame still rose to an all-time high because of my television debut. People recognized me everywhere I went. Star Search was one of the most highly viewed television shows at that time, so my name became quite familiar. Fast-forward, I felt the call to head to Atlanta to pursue my singing career as an R&B artist. I had been carrying this dream of singing since I was an adolescent. I remember distinctly, during my teen years, purchasing a car tag that read, "Born to Sing." Once I settled in Roswell Georgia, I found a studio producer and plunged into songwriting and recording. Several months later the Lord decided to invade my world and shift my dream of becoming the next "Ms. Whitney Houston."

Over a three-day period, the Lord really turned my life around. One morning while driving to work, I heard the voice of Holy Spirit (internally) ask me, "What are you going to do with your life?" It was so clear and profound in my spirit that it startled me. I was not afraid because the Lord is gentleman, but the voice was very distinct. Although I was not yet a believer, I knew it was the voice of the Lord.

After pondering the question, I mumbled softly, "Well, Lord, You know what I'm doing with my life...I am here to pursue my singing career." Holy Spirit said nothing in response. The next day, around the same time of my morning commute to work and almost at the same exact spot as the day before, the Lord asked me again, "What are you going to do with your life?" Okay, now I was getting extremely concerned at this point. I knew that the answer I had given Him the day before could not have been a sufficient answer, so that day, I don't think I answered Him at all...I just pondered the question all the way to work knowing that my world as I knew it was about to change.

At my job, there was a beautiful young lady by the name of Monica whom I knew was a believer because we had previously talked about her belief in God. I told Monica that I had heard the voice of the Lord on the way in, and she was so excited. Her countenance lit up like the sun in its fullness as I shared my morning encounter. It was very evident to her that God was doing a work in me, although I had not come to terms with what was happening.

The next morning around the same time, at the same location on the highway, the Lord asked me the same question again and I pondered the question in my heart all day. On the third morning, once again, Holy Spirit asked me what was I going to do with my life. I felt like Peter. Inadequate! I knew this was the call of surrender. I knew that life as I had lived it would be no more. When I arrived at work, I told Monica that I felt like the Lord was calling me to surrender my life to Him. I will never understand why this Holy Ghost arrest couldn't have happened in Raleigh, but maybe it was because I was in a place that I could hear God. Or maybe my sights were set for a path that was not ordained by God, so He intervened. Jesus knew how determined I was to make this dream a reality, and like Nimrod in Genesis 11, I was building my own tower of Babel and nothing was going to stop me from living my dream. Obviously my plans were different from His, and I'm glad He turned me around.

    When I returned to North Carolina, there was still a pull to sing with my old R&B, Top 40 band. Although others told me this was my "job" and that God would understand, something about their answer didn't quite settle with me. So, I decided to inquire of the Lord for His answer to this very controversial issue. I fasted and prayed for several days and asked God if it was okay to be a Christian and still sing secular songs in secular environments. I asked Him why was I feeling like it was not the right thing to do; to sing secular songs in places like night clubs and country clubs. He answered me ever so clearly! Here is the Lord's response to me, "Because it does not glorify Me." And there you have it! The struggle was over for me. No more wondering and listening to all of the different opinions of others and getting different answers to this important question. The Father had answered my question and I was satisfied with His response.

    I realize that there are still many people who struggle with this issue or may even disagree with me, but seek the Lord for yourself, just as I did.

Consecration has all to do with being set apart and I wanted to be totally set apart for the Father's use. I won't go into all of the dynamics of what singing secular music does to your spirit man, but this chapter is a call to come out of Babylon. You don't have to compromise and sing for the world in order to make money or to obtain notoriety. Jesus asked the question in Mark 8:36-37, "For what will it profit a man if he gains the whole world, and loses his own soul? Or what will a man give in exchange for his soul?" God provides for His children and He will never ask you to compromise who you are for money or fame. The Lord has blessed me immeasurably since then, and I've been singing for Him ever since. Do I have any regrets? Absolutely not! If you sing or play for money, then money will become your god or your baal. God gave you that gift and talent and ability to glorify Him and one day, you will have to give an account for how you utilized it, so use it to His glory.

    In this hour and season, we as a nation and a church are at a tipping point. God is saying to His bride, come out of everything that is and has the potential to be false. Bitter and sweet waters cannot flow from the same fountain. A good tree cannot bear bad fruit and a bad tree cannot bear good fruit.

    America is at a crossroads. Will she once again embrace the God of her fathers or will she embrace the ways of mystery Babylon? Will she deny the very motto stamped on every United States paper currency that says, "In God We Trust," or will she once again turn to God and repent for her iniquity, transgressions and sins? In 1 Kings 18:21, Elijah asked the people, "How long will you falter between two opinions? If the LORD is God, follow Him; but if Baal, follow him." How long will God's people jump back and forth between two positions? How long will they mingle holy with unholy? How long will they reject truth? How long will they compromise? Jesus told the church at

Laodicea in Revelation 3:15 that He wished they would be either cold or hot but because they will be indecisive, neither hot or cold, He will vomit (spue) her out of His mouth.

Mystery Babylon is alive and well! Many Christians and Jews are already losing their lives in the name of religion by malicious radicals. Here's what Isaiah 5:20 says, "Woe to those who call evil good and good evil, who change darkness into light and light into darkness, who change bitter into sweet and sweet into bitter!" (CJB). Isaiah pronounced a woe of judgment upon such people. We are called to be salt and light, a people of truth, a people of courage and a people of integrity. We are not called to blend in or to look like the world in an effort to draw the world or try to lower the standards of the Kingdom in order to draw the masses. Unless the Father draws an individual, no one will be drawn to Him! "No man can come to me, except the Father which hath sent me draw him: and I will raise him up at the last day," (John 6:44 KJV). Trying to become like the world in order to draw the world to Christ is the work of the enemy and the works of flesh. We are called to be salt and light while allowing Holy Spirit to move and operate through us. Holy Spirit does the work…not us.

When you operate in your Kingdom identity, the God within you will draw men. Extend love and not strife. Pray for others rather than condemn them. Kingdom principles are different from worldly principles. In Revelation 18, the angel of the Lord is talking to believers. Come out of anything that appears idolatrous, religious, immoral or biblically questionable. Find credible godly counselors and become accountable to them, for there is safety in many advisers (Proverbs 11:14 CJB). Paul says in Romans 6:13, "And do not offer any part of yourselves to sin as an instrument for wickedness. On the contrary, offer yourselves to God as people alive from the dead, and your various parts to God as instruments for righteousness," (CJB). When you give over parts of your body to sin or Babylon, it becomes an instrument of wickedness. When you willfully disobey, you are giving your body over to unrighteousness. Because of Christ, you now have the power to overcome, so it is up to you to exercise that power. Disregard for the truth is a segway to demonic deception. The Word of the Lord is and will always be the great plumb line. You have been called to come out of belief systems and practices that are not in alignment with God's Word. You must declare that Babylon will not rule over you because you are a citizen of a better city, the Jerusalem above (Galatians 4:26).

How can you avoid embracing the ways of Babylon? First, you must identify teachings, mindsets, or beliefs that are contrary to the Word of God because such teaching abolish and/or minimize the authority of God's Word. You must also be careful of self-deception. The Pharisees fooled themselves into thinking they were the only recipients of salvation and everyone else was lost. They did not understand the scriptures. Make sure that what you believe and hold as truth agrees with God's Word and His will. God is not obligated to do or fulfill anything contrary to His Word or His nature or His will. God's Word or His standards have NOT changed.

Secondly, you can avoid becoming a victim of Satan's deception by communing with God daily. When you commune with the Lord, you pray and talk to Him, you listen for His voice, you sing to Him, and you meditate on His Word. You must allow Holy Spirit to saturate your heart with His presence. Is all of this necessary in order to walk in your true identity? Yes! Amos says in chapter 3:3, "Can two walk together, unless they are agreed?" Can you truly walk with Christ without understanding His ways? When you are able to understand and walk in His ways, you are able to walk in His authority. When you commune with Him, He transforms you and causes your thoughts to align with His. Holy Spirit will lead and guide you through every situation of life if you will hear His voice and follow His lead.

Thirdly, you must continue to abide in Christ. 1 John 2:6 says, "He who says he abides in Him ought himself also to walk just as He walked." Jesus said in John 15:4 to abide in Him and He would abide in us. The word abide is the Greek word meno and one of its definitions means, "to continue to be present; to remain as one, not to become another or different." The way you keep yourself shielded from falsehood is to be ever-present with Holy Spirit and allow Him to lead you on a daily basis. This point ties in with the second but requires an intentional and constant abiding in Christ. You must make every effort to stay close to the Lord and be a disciple of His Word. Make every effort to become a good steward of your time, talent, and treasure. Make every effort to love the Lord God with all your heart and have no other gods before Him. You must endeavor to keep a pure heart, love God's people, serve God's people, and be that light that sits upon a hill that cannot be hidden (Matthew 5:14).

The fourth way to avoid deception is to be on guard. We are told that false teachers and/or prophets will come posing as legitimate religious teachers. Paul identified them as false apostles, deceitful workers, transforming themselves into apostles of Christ (2 Corinthians 11:13). Godly discernment is a powerful tool and gift for the believer, so if you need more of it, pray, ask the Father, and believe that you receive it. Deception is always mixed with a tiny portion of truth. You will need the wisdom, knowledge and revelation of God to shield you from the poison of deception.

In summary, you and I must have nothing to do with Babylon. Do you think it's ironic that just recently, a replica of the tower of Babel was erected in

London? Plans to erect the tower in New York in April were postponed so let's keep our eyes open to see what future plans will be. Babylon represents idolatry, rebellion against God and His Word, witchcraft, disobedience, selfishness, greed and unfaithfulness, to name a few. Flee any and everything with suspicious motives and intents that pretentiously offer false humility, status, financial prosperity, and security.

Also be careful not to set up idols in your own heart. Avoid worshiping people or things. It is easy to become distracted and exalt things like, careers, pursuits, children, and yourself in the place of God. We are all enticed and drawn away by our own desires when we do not renew our minds daily and bring our flesh under subjection to the Father. Babylon is the utter seat of malicious deception and perversion, and it defies anything that represents holiness and God. Babylon will entice many by appealing to their wayward or selfish desires by offering counterfeit security, notoriety, and religious freedom. Many will become intoxicated with the wine of her trickery, but the call to the church today is to "Come out of Babylon!"

This is a wake-up call. This is the sound of the shofar blasting throughout the camp warning of impending danger. Get up warriors, put on your heavenly armor and prepare to do battle in the spirit. Pray without ceasing. Cover your church, your leaders, your home, your children, and everything you own with prayer. Stay close to Jesus. Listen for Holy Spirit's voice and promptings. Pay attention to world and current events and pray for Heavenly intervention and divine interception. Worship the Lord in the spirit of holiness. Honor the Lord in all you do and make Him first in your life. Go back to your first love, to the things you did when you first believed. Run swiftly to the arms of Jesus, for He promises never to leave you nor forsake you! Grace covers you as you align yourself in word and in deed. Remain underneath the Chuppah of Abba Daddy. David said in Psalm 24:3-5, "Who may ascend into the hill of the LORD? Or who may stand in His holy place? He who has clean hands and a pure heart, Who has not lifted up his soul to an idol, Nor sworn deceitfully. He shall receive blessing from the LORD, And righteousness from the God of his salvation." Having clean hands refers to your actions and having pure hearts refers to your motives and intents. Old habits must die in order to transition into your new season. Pursue peace and crucify the deeds of the flesh. Refuse to be governed by your emotions and untrained senses. Your spirit man always wants to do what's right so live in the Spirit so that you may walk in oneness with the Lord.

You have greatness inside of you! Set your heart to reject the ways of Babylon at all cost. You are about to enter your promised land! Israel could not take her old ways, neither the ways of the Canaanites, into the Promised Land. The medium of exchange is your life for His. Jesus has set you free from Babylon, from bondage. You are a victor in every way. Choose to live in His divine freedom. Make the declaration of Joshua today, "As for me and my house, we will serve the LORD," (Joshua 24:15).

CHAPTER FOUR

In Christ

"Therefore, if anyone is in Christ, he is a new creation; old things have passed away; behold, all things have become new."
2 Corinthians 5:17

In the previous chapters of this book, I pray that I have made it clear that you are awesomely made in God's image and made free by the blood of the Lamb. I hope that I have also stressed the importance of living a godly life by removing the baals of bondage and compromise. In continuing your quest to understanding your identity IN CHRIST, I feel this chapter is very important because it will establish a firm and sure foundation.

Because there are so many denominations and religious beliefs, I can see how babes in Christ are easily confused. I've heard people make comments like, "Well Muslims call him Allah and Christians call him God, but it's all the same God." This is the biggest fabrication of the day. Any religion that does not believe that Jesus the Christ is the Son of God does not serve the same God as Christians. There is no Christianity without Jesus, so failure to believe in Jesus (his birth, death and resurrection), means our God is not the same as theirs. There are a litany of names listed in the Bible for God, but Joseph Smith, Allah, Budda or Krishna, just to name a few, are not His names. Further, our God is not a God of hate, war, and murder. The very essence of our God is love and this characteristic about Him is what sets Him apart. Abba's nature does not change regardless of what we think or have been indoctrinated.

Your Identity in Christ

I want to talk about what it means to be IN Christ because a lot of people want to be AROUND Christ but not IN Christ. When you come to the full understanding of what it means to be IN Christ, then and only then can you walk in your true identity in Christ. After all, our Identity is embedded in Him. In 2 Corinthians 5:17, the preposition "in" is the Greek word "en", and it denotes "a fixed position in place, time or state." According to the Blueletter Bible Greek Lexicon, "en" also means "a relation of rest; united." When you accept Jesus as Lord AND Savior, there is a joining or infusion that takes place. That is, the Spirit of Christ comes to dwell within you. God writes His law in your heart and His Spirit takes up residence there. John 6:30 says that the Spirit gives life and Romans 8:9 states that you do not belong to Christ if you do not have the Spirit of Christ, and if Christ is in you, the body is dead because of sin, but the Spirit is life because of righteousness. The same Spirit that gave Jesus the power to overcome the law of death lives within you and gives you power to overcome everything you will ever face in life. Christ wants you joined to Him, so that He can reveal Himself to the world through you.

To be in Christ also means that you have surrendered your will to Him. We must all heed the call of Matthew 16:24 by denying ourselves, taking up our cross and following Him. According to the Blueletter Greek Lexicon, to deny means "to forget one's self, to lose sight of one's self and one's own interest." Now how far to the left is this concept in today's society? We see more "selfies" today than anything else. Even the Pope was captured taking selfies during his visit to the United States. In the Kingdom of God, it's all about being selfless. Jesus was selfless in everything He did. He gave all glory to the Father and never sought to be a celebrity. He did nothing for notoriety or fame. He prayed in secret and at times healed individuals and told them to tell no one. He was never plagued with pride and haughtiness. His desire was always to do the will of His Father and finish His work, according to John 4:34. The Kingdom of God operates by a different set of principles, and as a Kingdom citizen, you operate under different orders.

Salvation is the first step of being in Christ. As you mature, it is essential that you strive to make love your utmost priority because God operates purely by love. Jesus said if you love Him, then you are to keep His commandments because these commandments lead to eternal love and eternal life. It should never burdensome to follow someone you love. I can remember when I met my spouse; we were head over hills for each other. Whatever he did was okay with me. Nothing mattered more than our being together. Well, it should be the same with Jesus. The more time you spend with Him, the less you should want to leave Him. The reason I love worship so much is because I get to sing to the lover of my soul and enter into His divine presence where He shares His heart for me and with me. It is a place of intimacy and it is reserved for all of Abba's children.

To be in Christ, you must forsake all, even yourself. Let me rephrase that. To be in Christ, you must forsake all, ESPECIALLY yourself. You can no longer be at the top of your priority list. Christ has to be at the top. Denying yourself is difficult because you are taught and trained just the opposite. You are told to discover yourself, do what you feel, love yourself above all. This way of thinking is self-centered. You are taught to hold yourself in higher esteem than others and reach for the stars and to do other me, me, me-centered stuff. I have learned in this Christian journey that the more humble, abased, transparent, selfless, and invisible I become, the more fragrant my life is. Again, my friends, the Kingdom of God operates on totally different principles, and we must reshape the way we think in order to be representatives for Christ.

To be in Christ also requires intimate fellowship, a necessity for walking in life as a new creation in Him. This journey with Christ requires maturation, and maturation comes from fellowshipping with Christ. . A metamorphosis has to take place. All things must become new. You are a beautiful blossoming flower that must reach full bloom. Just as a child must go through child development in this natural life, you must also go through spiritual development. If you have been saved for any amount of time, you should be able to look back to when you first gave your life to Christ and detect some major maturing; and if not, "Houston we have a problem!" The more you study His word, the more you worship, the more you pray, the more you overcome trials in your life, the more mature you become. It is imperative that every believer develops a lifestyle of intimacy with Jesus. I like the teaching by Graham Cooke in The Kind Intentions of God where he says, "God doesn't just want visitation, He wants habitation." Holy Spirit wants to live with you and in you through the vehicle of communing. His desire is to train your ear to hear His voice. He wants to teach you the things of Heaven and intimate fellowship is the pathway to habitation.

In the 15th chapter of John, Jesus talks a lot about abiding in Him. Jesus said if we remain connected to Him, He would remain connected to us. Notice how this is conditional. In verse 16 of John 15 Jesus said "if" anyone does not abide in Him so this means that we are all given a choice to abide or not to abide. Being connected to someone is more than just reading about them, and knowing of them. It deals with intimacy, spending time in their presence, getting to know what they like and dislike. Knowing and experiencing God goes way beyond just reading about Him or reading about

His ways. We must get to the point where we are joined together with Him and partnering in His plan for humanity. This means you read His Word but you also listen for His voice through His Word and also through His still small voice, which comes in many ways.

      Holy Spirit wants to woo you into greater intimacy. There is no way you and I can be IN Christ without intimately knowing Him and being known by Him. You must be sincere about becoming a friend of God. Intimacy with Christ must be a priority. You must carve out time to be alone with Him. Set the atmosphere. Play prophetic or soaking worship music that will prepare and set the atmosphere. Read His word. Sit and meditate on His words and to the words of the songs. Do as Hebrews 12:2 instructs and fix your spiritual eyes on Jesus. Let Him be the center of your thoughts. Pray in the Spirit. Sit before His presence and pray until you feel the wooing of Holy Spirit, and when that happens, let Holy Spirit take the lead. There are many ways to enter the presence of the Lord, but start somewhere. Be calculated about going before Abba Daddy and hearing what He has to say. He loves you and wants to spend intimate, quiet time with YOU. There are strategies and plans He has for you and communing with Him is the place to obtain those strategies.

      To be in Christ requires obedience. An important scripture to meditate on is John 15:10 (ESV) where Jesus says, "If you keep my commandments, you will abide in my love, just as I have kept my Father's commandments and abide in His love." Obedience is so key in the Kingdom of God. All throughout the bible, angels were always obedient to God and to their assignment. While we know that we are not under the stringent laws and rules of the Old Testament, we are still compelled to follow God's Word and His ways. If you are going to walk in your true identity in Christ, obedience must be your highest attribute. You obey because you love and because you love, you obey.

    To obey simply means to comply or to carry out or to submit to authority. As a Kingdom citizen, you submit to the authority of King Jesus, and set your heart to carry out His plans for your life. Does that mean you will not be able to pursue the things you desire? Absolutely not! Does the Lord need people in the marketplace? Absolutely! It is up to you to discover the Lord's will for you and pursue it. His desire will be intertwined with yours, which will stir your desire even the more to fulfill His purposes.

    Abiding in Christ means knowing and honoring His Word. The phrase "abide in us" means that we honor and cherish God's Word above all else. Paul tells us in 2 Timothy 2:15 to be diligent to present yourself approved to God, a worker who doesn't need to be ashamed, correctly handling the Word of truth. This means you and I are called to expound on the word correctly, but you're first called to understand and apply the word to your own personal life. Psalm 119:11 says, "Your word I have hidden in my heart, That I might not sin against You." The word of God is life. The more you consume it, the more of His life you experience. When temptations arise, it is the Word of God tucked away in your heart that will give you the power to overcome. No Word in your heart...no power to overcome. It is God's Word that has power over the enemy. His Word is life breathing and sharper than any two-edged sword, but it will be useless if not applied. God's Word will never return to Him void (Isaiah 55:11) so when you use it according to His purposes, He brings His Word to pass.

    Is it difficult to adhere to some of God's word? Yes! For example, it is difficult to forgive when someone has offended or intentionally hurt you. But there are consequences, like a hardened heart, for not forgiving, so I would rather do as the word instructs and forgive so that I, too, can be forgiven. God's Word brings liberty to you. His Word frees you from spiritual bondage. Yes, it is a process, and yes it is difficult at times, but that's why you have Holy Spirit to help you get through difficult situations. And guess what? He is faithful to see you through every difficult situation, trial, sickness, or whatever may come your way! This is where you grow in your intimacy with Christ. This is where you grow in faith. Abiding in the Word of God keeps you on the right path. The more you allow your flesh to submit to the rule of God's Word, the closer you are drawn into Him.

    As I mentioned earlier, one of the definitions for abide is to continue to remain. One thing I have learned as a worship leader over many years is the importance of abiding. There has to be a continual denying of self and a clinging to Christ. You cannot lead people where you have not gone. I have seen an epic failure in our praise and worship events and services today due to a lack of transparency. It is difficult to lead a congregation in worship if you have not been there yourself. Worship service is not the time for you to shine! Leading worship on Sundays should be an extension of private, weekly worship.

    How do you remain in Christ on your job? By listening for His still small voice while working; by giving Him thanks in all things; by helping your coworkers in their times of need. You remain in Him by taking opportunities to pray throughout the day. You also abide in Christ by seeking answers from Him before making difficult decisions. You remain in Christ by waiting to get His perspective on a matter or event and being careful not to judge anyone or anything prematurely. Am I asking you to be legalistic? No. I am simply saying that these are the things you should do effortless because they are extensions of your intimate, daily fellowship with the Lord.

Your Identity in Christ

A big part of being in Christ is being set apart for His purposes. Your identity is tied into your purpose. Everything you need is wrapped up in your identity. As you set your affections on Him (Colossians 3:1-2), you come into alignment with Heaven's agenda for you. Your life is now hidden with Christ in Heaven, and once you come to the full realization of this, you must value, judge, view, and consider everything from an eternal and heavenly perspective. One of the most revelatory Scriptures to me says that we have died and our lives are hidden with the Messiah in God, (Colossians 3:3). Watchman Nee states in his book, The Spiritual Man, that "When Christ was judged, all who will be regenerated were present in Christ. His judgment is hence taken as their judgment, and all who have believed in Christ shall no longer be judged." Although you and I were yet to be born or even saved when Jesus walked the earth, because God knew that we would accept Jesus as Lord and Savior, when Jesus was judged, we were also judged and acquitted! That's the power of the blood, the cross, grace and mercy! Romans 3:24 says that you are "justified freely by His grace through the redemption that is in Christ Jesus." This is why there is salvation in no other name but Jesus. No other deity or god has given its life for the sake of mankind...NONE! And even if they have claimed otherwise, they are false. "Sin as a whole and our own sins were judged, therefore it has no power over those who have joined to the Lord's death and who have condemned it in their flesh," (Nee, 1997).

God has imparted and breathed His life (zoe) into your spirit man. Your spirit has been restored to its original position of authority. Holy Spirit within you causes your spirit to be in-tune with the spiritual realm, the realm of God. Now don't get me wrong, you can be an unbeliever and tap into the spirit realm, but the biggest question to answer is, "Who or what is your source?" Satan wants nothing more than for people to tap into the spirit world but from the dark side. He can give you information and allow you to have spiritual encounters, but they are from him, not Jesus. Today more than ever, it disturbs my spirit to the core when I see all of these television shows for kids that are deeply rooted in witchcraft, satanism and the like, so be watchful and careful with what you allow your children to watch on television or listen to on the radio.

Another key to abiding in Christ is understanding that you have been crucified with Christ, therefore, there is now no condemnation. The eternal death sentence has been obliterated because of the blood of Jesus. Paul says in Galatians 2:20, "I have been crucified with Christ; it is no longer I who live, but Christ lives in me; and the life which I now live in the flesh I live by faith in the Son of God, who loved me and gave Himself for me." Did you read that? Paul considered his flesh crucified with Christ's. He stated that he would no longer live according to the dictates of his flesh, but the new life he was currently living was through the power of Christ.

It is imperative that you fully embrace the work of the cross. The cross is where the death sentence for humanity was judged and a judgment rendered in your favor. Your old nature must continually be nailed to the cross. Nee said, "If the flesh is to be kept confined to the place of a curse, we must be watchful always. The flesh must never be offered any ground. Even with conversing with others, you need to be on alert lest in many words the flesh is equipped to perform its works" (1997). The cross is where the victory was won!

I recently went through a battle against my thought life and dealing with my flesh. I had started to criticize needlessly and it slowly progressed to murmuring and complaining and fault-finding. It wasn't long before I began justifying my criticisms. The battle became so intense that the enemy was constantly showing me things to complain about against a particular person. This went on for months, and it was starting to take a toll on the relationship. Finally, one day I had had enough. I knew the enemy was attempting to destroy my relationship with this person and striving to rend my heart through disappointment. He was trying to destroy my marriage because it was my husband that I was constantly murmuring and complaining about. Although I was not complaining to him directly, my thoughts were complaining about him (what he wasn't doing) and I could feel the wedge of division setting in.

One day while at home, I was watching a video of a young girl from Africa who had major encounters with Jesus. One of the things she said really caught my attention because I had heard it before. She said that in the realm of the spirit, thoughts are the medium of communication. She said that our thoughts appear before God like words or vibrations flashing on a big television screen. While I understood that God knew my thoughts, it was what she said about HOW He sees them that really jolted me. She said that all of our thoughts appear before Him as on an open screen. I knew that I had to end the raging mind battle of criticism because to know that my ungodly thoughts were appearing before Heaven as on an open screen, staggered me. I didn't want thoughts of bitterness and complaining running before the Father so I knew I had to deal with my mind right away.

That day I cried out to the Lord for forgiveness. I did not focus on anyone but myself. I repented for not casting down accusations the enemy presented about my husband. I repented of not thinking and dwelling on the positive but focusing on the negative. I began to bind the spirit of divorce (although that never crossed my mind at all) and refused to let the enemy contaminate my mind and destroy our relationship. I prayed in the spirit (tongues) and with the understanding (English) until I felt a release. I knew that in order to walk in victory, I could not allow the enemy to win the battle over my mind. I quoted and meditated on several scriptures dealing with thinking the right thoughts and only speaking words of affirmation. The main scripture that kept me grounded was Matthew 12:37 which says, "For by your words you will be justified, and by your words you will be condemned." The Lord heard my cry and delivered me that day. I felt the peace of Abba upon me, and I knew God had heard my case and vindicated me. The enemy could no longer oppress me because I had confessed and surrendered. The enemy is always looking for a crack or an open door. Because I entertained thoughts of fault-finding and complaining, I became consumed with negative thoughts. But God is faithful! Holy Spirit showed me the way of escape, and I took it! Please don't ever think that unspoken thoughts are hidden from God. Everything is open before Him, so keep the enemy at bay by dispelling soulish thoughts about yourself or anyone else.

Being in Christ gives you the ability to overcome. You are an overcomer. Revelation 12:11 (KJV) says, "And they overcame him by the blood of the Lamb, and by the word of their testimony; and they loved not their lives unto the death." You overcome the enemy when you understand the power of the testimony of the cross….the power of the blood of Jesus! You overcome when you identify with Jesus' death and when you identify with His resurrection. When you testify of your redemption through the blood of Jesus, you overcome. In the days to come, those believers who will be persecuted and accused by satan before God will overcome when they testify of what the blood has done for them. In the days ahead, you must operate in your Kingdom identity. Satan will test you to see not only if you know who you are, but also tempt you to see if you will walk in the level of authority you possess.

Being IN Christ is all about positioning. You have moved from slaves to sons, from enemies to friends. Don't believe the voices in the world attempting to exalt their gods and prophets to the same position as Jesus. You have been adopted into the Kingdom as sons of God, which is why you can now call Him Abba Daddy. Because you are a child and a mature son of God, you are an heir together with Christ IF you share His suffering along with His glory. When you find yourself in the face of the enemy, cry out the names of other gods, then cry out the Name and blood of Jesus, and see which name the enemy responds to! Don't be fooled. Satan knows he's no match for Jesus and the blood that was poured out for humanity on the cross. It's the sacrificing of Jesus' life and His blood that has placed you back into the right position in God and His kingdom. This is why the Bible clearly says in Acts 4:12, "Nor is there salvation in any other, for there is no other name under heaven given among men by which we must be saved."

The enemy wants to steal your identity! He would love for you to walk through life aimlessly, forfeiting your Kingdom inheritance. In Acts 19, Holy Spirit was performing great miracles through Paul. Seven sons of Sceva, along with traveling Jewish exorcists, decided they would call the name of Jesus in an effort to cast out evil spirits over those who were possessed (verse 13). It was obvious they had no relationship with Jesus because they tried to cast out the evil spirits by the "Jesus whom Paul preached." The evil spirit responded to their futile efforts in verse 15 by saying, "And the evil spirit answered and said, 'Jesus I know, and Paul I know, but who are you?'" Did you get that? The evil spirit knew Jesus and Paul, but because the others had no relationship with Jesus, they had no authority over them. Therefore, the evil leapt upon them, overpowered them, and prevailed against them so that they fled from the house wounded and naked. One demon-possessed man was able to overpower approximately 8-10 men all because they were attempting to operate in an authority they did not have! Do you see that? It's not about power, but about position and authority in Christ! Even the enemies of God know who you are. You are a citizen of the Kingdom of God with legal rights and authority to wreak havoc on satan's kingdom. When you witness to nonbelievers or testify of God's goodness, you do damage to the kingdom of darkness!

      Being IN Christ means being partnered and joined with His death, His resurrection, His suffering, and His reigning. Don't settle for just hanging on the periphery of Christianity. If you are going to be saved, be sure to enjoy ALL of the benefits that come with being a citizen of the highest Kingdom. Enjoy total deliverance, total freedom, total healing, and total love! Because you are in Christ, you have also been called out to legislate spiritually for God. By legislating for God's Kingdom, you are extending His Kingdom government and influence on the earth. Your words have authority in Heaven and on earth, as long as you remain connected to the vine of Jesus Christ. You are God's governing force in the earth and have been given keys of authority from Him to legislate from the spiritual realm. With these keys, you are to close spiritual doors by which evil and destruction might otherwise enter. This is done in your personal life as well as the life of others. In Matthew 28:8 Jesus said that all authority had been given to Him in Heaven and on earth. The word authority is the Greek word "exousia" which is also the same word for power. Authority and power gives you the right to rule and govern in a particular position and jurisdiction. It also means having the right to make judicial decisions and having the authority to manage domestic affairs, to magistrate. Here's what satan told Jesus in the wilderness in Luke

4:6, "And the devil said to Him, 'All this authority I will give You, and their glory; for this has been delivered to me, and I give it to whomever I wish.'"

As I was studying and researching this topic on authority, I found there are many who don't believe that satan was given some element of authority after the fall. First, I would like you to think about how the Kingdom of God is based on a judicial system. If you search throughout the Scriptures, you will see that there are councils in Heaven (Ps. 82, 89; Job 1:6; Zechariah, Daniel 7). The councils on earth, such as the Sanhedrin, were established based upon the realities of the councils and assemblies that were already established in the Heavenly realm. Hebrews 11:3 clearly tells us that God created the visible from the invisible. The main idea is to understand that God's Kingdom is a judicial Kingdom, with a Judge, where God establishes and decides judgments and the fate of mankind. Psalm 82:1 clearly states that Elohim stands in the congregation or council of the mighty ones or gods.

You can legislate through prayer and by releasing God's Word. When you open your mouth and declare what thus says the Lord, you have Heaven's backing. Jesus said in Matthew 16:19, "And I will give you the keys to the kingdom of heaven, and whatever you bind on earth will be bound in heaven, and whatever you loose on earth will be loosed in heaven." The word bind has a legal connotation and it means "to put under obligation, of the law; to forbid; prohibit; declare to be illicit; unlawful." Jesus was saying that whatever you declare unlawful on earth, He will declare unlawful in Heaven. And this, my friend, is the key to the Kingdom. It is your ability to legislate, bind and loose, for Heaven on earth.

From my own personal experience, Holy Spirit is teaching me how to walk in Christ and release His Words in the earth. As I hear the Word of the Lord to give to others or to release in a particular environment, I move on what I hear. God speaks through nature as well, so I constantly analyze my surroundings and things in sight. I have changed the way I see myself. I ask Holy Spirit to give me the confidence I need to be effective for Him. I pray the Word with authority and faith and you can do the same by renewing your mind. When the Lord brought the Israelites out of the land of Egypt, He changed their identity. He took a people, who were not a people, and made them His people. He changed their name. He gave them an inheritance. You must not settle for anything less than your Kingdom identity. When you come to Christ, all of His fullness comes with Him. You are deeply rooted in Him, and His breath and His blood flows through you (Col. 2:19) because you are of His royal bloodline. Being IN Christ means more than just salvation. You have a position of royalty and inheritance. Now's the time to take your rightful position!

CHAPTER FIVE

Sonship: Your Kingdom Inheritance

"For as many as are led by the Spirit of God, these are sons of God. For you did not receive the spirit of bondage again to fear, but you received the Spirit of adoption by whom we cry out, 'Abba, Father.'"
Romans 8:14-15

Identity is the fabric of your spiritual existence. This chapter is the "secret weapon" of identity because it will unveil to you the essence of your existence. This chapter of discovery should revolutionize the way you see yourself from this day forward and when you fully understand how you have died with Christ and that you now live in Him, Holy Spirit can now begin to release strategies to you regarding how to live your everyday life in total victory and alignment with the Father's purpose.

One of the main focuses going forward should be that of humility. Numbers 12:3 says that Moses was more humble than all men who were on the face of the earth. James 4:6 says, "But He gives more grace. Therefore He says: 'God resists the proud, But gives grace to the humble.'" Everything we do for God must be motivated and undergirded in humility. Let's be very clear; the more God gives you, the more humble you must become. The Father will not share His glory with anyone, so the key to partnering with Christ and doing marvelous exploits for the Kingdom of God is to have a humble heart. We know that Jesus was the most humble person to walk the earth and He was God. He humbled Himself, left His eternal home in Heaven to put on flesh, and carried out a mandate that demanded being mutilated on a degrading cross. Proverbs 18:12 says that humility precedes honor. If you want to be honored, humility is the prerequisite. Jesus humbled Himself; therefore, His Father honored Him above all. The Word tells us that God exalts the humble, so the way up is down!

I believe the church is at the brink of her finest hour. I honestly do not believe that Jesus will return and find His bride feeble, destitute, and shrieking under moral decay and divisiveness; rather, she will be without spot or wrinkle, glorious and holy. In order for this to happen, I believe the church is about to experience a great awakening, and once this awakening happens, the true sons of God will manifest and carry out Kingdom orders. So ladies, sorry to be the bearer of bad news, but you are a son. The Kingdom of God is not relegated to gender, so it's okay to be called a son. Men, guess what? You are brides, so I can really see the humor of God in all of this. Most importantly, as a woman, I embrace who I am as a son of God!

So why was Jesus called the Son of God? Why was He called the Son of man? He could have easily been called King or Prophet or Priest of God, which He was, so why was there an emphasis on being a "Son" of God. John 3:16 says, "For God so loved the world that He gave His only begotten Son, that whoever believes in Him should not perish but have everlasting life." Jesus was the only one of His kind. Begotten denotes singularity in kind. There was/is no one like Christ. He existed from the beginning and was not created like man and everything that exists came through Him. He has no beginning or end. Now, did God need a son to carry out His will? Could Jesus have come as a king and satisfied the judgment upon man, which was the belief of the Pharisees and Jews of that day. They were looking for a conquering king. They were looking for a powerful king who would rid them of their present Roman oppression and servitude.

In studying the principles of a Kingdom, kingship can only be inherited by a son. In biblical times and still in countries today, a prince (a son) is someone who is in the direct bloodline or position of the present king. A prince can never take the throne as king unless he is an heir...either by being a direct descendant or an adopted son of his father, unless otherwise agreed. Every kingdom has a king and the desire of every king is for his son to succeed his throne and rule at the expiration of his term or life. Only a son, either biologically or legally, can inherit his father's throne.

In order for Christ to reign as King, He had to first become a son. In order to fulfill prophetic scripture and inherit David's earthly throne forever, He had to become the Son. In order to reign as King over earth and Heaven's Kingdom, He had to be of the same essence and bloodline as God the Father and man also. Being a son has everything to do with relationship, bloodline, legality and authority. Jesus was of the DNA of Heaven and of man, but His bloodline was never tainted by sin. He carried in His being the DNA of the Father and the DNA genetic makeup of man, yet He walked in perfect oneness with the Father. In Heaven, flesh and blood does not exist. Flesh and blood are needed to sustain life on planet earth. Jesus left eternity temporarily and clothed Himself in human flesh in order to legitimate what Adam had forfeited. Satan did all he could to annihilate the coming of the Messiah: from the murder of Abel by the hands of his brother Cain, to the killing of the male children during the days of Moses, to his malicious attempt through Herod to thwart God's divine plan of His coming Son by murdering the children of Bethlehem and all the surrounding coastlands from the ages of two years old and younger. So it is clear, satan does understand inheritance. He understands legality. He knows there's nothing he can do with believers who know who they are in Christ. He trembles at those who walk in their rightful inheritance. Why do you think he fights so hard to entangle your children while they are young? Jesus makes it clear in John 10:10 that the thief comes for no other reason but to steal, kill and destroy, but He came to give you "zoe", the God kind of life. It is statan's ultimate plight to rob you of any kind of kingdom living and inheritance you have been legally granted.

Here's a quick testimony of how the enemy made an entrance into my life when I was a child in an attempt to rob me of my Kingdom inheritance and identity. I can't recall exactly the year, but many of you are probably familiar with the movie, The Exorcist. Well, for some reason, we were allowed to watch this nefarious movie that methodically opened a dark spiritual door. After watching the movie, I was mortified. I would go to bed every night fearful to shut off the lights for fear that some dreaded evil being would show up in my room. I would jump in bed and immediately cover up my head until I finally drifted off to sleep. It was not long afterwards that I began to really sense a dark presence in our room. My younger sister and I shared a room and I never shared my eerie suspicions with her.

If you have children, then I know you understand that children and youth are able to discern and see the spiritual things and beings a lot easier than adults. Well, let me tell you, I could discern the dark presence. I knew there was something very evil in my room, and it was there to scare and torment me. It was the spirit of fear that had made an entrance and was feeding off of the fears initiated by the movie. Every night I would feel this torturing spirit in my room. It never tried to do anything to me, so I guess it was there just to keep me in a state of fear and torment.

Many years later and after I gave my life to the Lord, one night as I lay down to sleep, I had a pretty terrifying encounter. My husband had to work overnight and as I rested on my back in bed, suddenly I felt my shoulders pinned to the bed and a silhouette of an entity was straddled over me pinning me down (please don't think I'm crazy or making this up or it was my imagination). I could not move or speak. My thoughts were the only things that were not paralyzed by this maleficent presence. Here's what it said to me, "Remember how I used to torture you as a little girl?" I could not say a word but in my mind I started shouting, "The blood of Jesus is against you. The blood of Jesus is against you!" I started trying to release myself from the grips of this wicked reprobate. As I fought to gain some type of footing, my words were released and I began to plead the blood of Jesus boldly and with extreme authority during this encounter. As soon as I was able to do this, the spirit left and I have not sensed or had to deal with it in that way again.

      Why am I sharing all of this? Because you must understand that your eyes, ears, mouth, hands and nose are gateways. What you allow to enter your gateways have access to either oppress you or bless you. Satan wants God's inherited sons. He wants to strip you of your inherited rights and keep you in some form of bondage, whether it be physically, mentally or emotionally. As a child, I wasn't sure if what I was experiencing was real or just a figment of my imagination, but the spirit of fear made it very plain to me later in life that it was not my imagination and it had been there torturing me for many years. I also wanted to stress to parents the importance of monitoring what you allow your children to watch on television and the music they listen to. There is a spirit world (good and bad) out there, and you can unknowingly introduce your children to unnecessary harm. The eyes are the windows to the soul or to say it as the Message Bible says (Matthew 6:22), "Your eyes are windows into your body." When you fill your eyes with light and truth, your body will be full of light and truth. If you fill them with other things, dark things, your body will be subject to the darkness you have presented to it.

Another interesting caveat to this story is that as my sister and I were talking about our childhood days just a few years ago, we discovered that she was having the exact same experience as me. Remember that I said we shared a room? This same dark spirit of fear that was torturing me was doing the same to her! The sad thing about it was that we both were too afraid to tell our mom or each another. So parents, ask your children questions. Ask them how they feel at bedtime. Ask them if they are afraid and if so, why? Also, turn off all televisions at night and leave worship music playing in your child(ren's) rooms or throughout the house. You can play scripture while you sleep. We must deal with fears and dark things through spiritual means.

When Jesus told Nicodemus in John 3:3 that he had to be born again, Nicodemus immediately tried to understand with the natural mind. He could not understand spiritual realities with a carnal understanding. Jesus had to go on and explain that the new birth had nothing to do with being born physically, but had all to do with being reborn spiritually. The new birth is granted to all who receive Jesus and are infused with His divine life. Ask Holy Spirit to continue to open your eyes to see things from a spiritual perspective.

Now let's talk more about what it means for you to be a son of God. Romans 8:14 says that all who are led by the Holy Spirit are God's sons. Led is the Greek word "ago" and it means, "to lay hold of; guided; directed; moved; influenced; driven." To be totally led by Holy Spirit means first receiving Him at salvation, being baptized in and by Him, and surrendering to His Lordship. It means having your everyday life led by Holy Spirit. It means listening for His promptings. It means spending time in prayer and fellowship with Him. It means allowing Him the ability to correct you when necessary and following His lead. The word adoption in verse 15 is the Greek word "huiothesia." Huios means "a son" and thesis means "a placing," and together they signify the place and condition of a son given to one to whom it does not naturally belong (Greek Lexicon).

As a believer, sonship has been bestowed upon you through adoption, and Holy Spirit helps you realize this sonship and the attitude you should have as sons. Slaves have no right to inheritance, but sons do, so it was imperative that Jesus qualified you as a son of God. A son deals with positioning and denotes an existing state. God the Father has placed you in the position of son and gave you the ability or right, through His Spirit, to exist legally as a son upon the earth. Jesus did not leave you an orphan. He made you a true son, whereby, making you a rightful inheritor. Although we know that Romans 8:23 talks about a yet future adoption, when our bodies will be redeemed, Paul says in Ephesians 1:5 that God the Father determined in advance that, through Jesus Christ, you and I would be His sons.

It is imperative that you first understand what it means to be a son and how you became a son. Now that you are a son, you have a new family, a new Father, a new Elder Brother, a new position, a new inheritance and a yet to come, new name. You have been engrafted into the family of the God, the Kingdom of God. God the Father is your new Father instead of satan, the god of this world. Jesus is your Elder Brother (Hebrews 2:11-12), and Heaven is your new final destination. Eternal life is one benefit of your inheritance, and sonship is your new position. Your filthy garments have been removed, and you now wear a robe of righteousness. Because you died with Christ, RIGHT NOW you are seated with Him in heavenly places (Ephesians 2:6). You now have the distinct privilege of living in the best of two worlds. Jesus came to this world to reveal or manifest the Kingdom of God. The veil has been removed, and now you and I can participate in the spiritual things of the Kingdom of God, as well as the things of the earth.

Genealogy is important in the Jewish culture. Jesus came through the line of David by means of Mary, who was a descendent of Abraham (read the genealogies in Matthew and Luke). The atoning and redemptive work of Jesus engrafted us, Gentiles, into the family of God where you and I have been adopted as sons. In Romans 11 beginning at verse 16, Paul uses the imagery of a tree and branches to unfold the mystery and wisdom of God's redemptive work through Christ. At first he said if the first piece of the lump is holy then the entire lump is holy, and if the root of a tree is holy, then the branches are holy. The root represents the life system of any tree and if the root is holy, so are the branches. Paul was explaining to the Gentiles that if the root system of the original faith of the Israelites is holy and acceptable, then the foundation which the apostles built upon is also holy. In verse 17 Paul discussed how some of the branches were being cut off, but not all of them. Because of their rejection of Jesus as Messiah and their disobedience, the Israelites have been temporarily cut off, but this is only happening to give the Gentiles an opportunity to become a part of the family of God. Grafted means "to cut off for the sake of inserting a scion; to inoculate; graft in." In dealing with plants, to engraft means to insert for propagation and propagation means to multiply. God took of his original tree (trees always represent family, descendants, etc.) or people (the Israelites) and has made or grafted us (Gentiles) into one new humanity whereby He is multiplying His children. Instead of His Kingdom belonging exclusively to Israel, it includes all who believe and will come to believe in His Son Jesus Christ. We know that the Israelites are destined for eternal salvation, but thanks be unto God for giving the Gentiles an opportunity to come into His Kingdom!

Let's now talk about what it means to be a mature son. Children do not remain children forever; at some point they grow up and mature. Just as we pass through the various stages of child development, I pray that no one remains a babe in Christ forever; you must move on into mature sonship. Although your DNA has already been written by God for your natural body, your spiritual growth is totally dependent upon you; your will, determination and obedience. Right now there are a lot of children in the body of Christ but not many sons. 1 Peter 2:1-2 says that as babes we, the body of Christ, should desire or thirst for the sincere milk of the Word so that we might grow by it. As your thirst for God is satisfied, you will grow into a mature son who's able to handle the meat of the Word. In Hebrews 5:13, Paul says that anyone who drinks milk is still a babe and has no experience in applying the Word of righteousness. Righteousness deals with the way or condition acceptable and approved by God. One main understanding of righteousness is that you no longer have to work, perform good deeds, or follow rituals in order to obtain salvation. The sacrifice of Jesus was enough to satisfy the judgment set against mankind and faith in Jesus and His atoning work puts you back in right standing with God. It is by faith that you freely receive and accept Jesus' righteousness and not your own. There is nothing you can do on your own to obtain righteousness; Jesus did and paid it all! Hallelujah!

The more you grow in the scriptures, the more mature you should become in applying it to your daily life and the more you apply it, the more understanding and wisdom you gain of Abba's ways and how to operate in His Kingdom. But let me say that reading the Word alone won't do it. You must depend on Holy Spirit to teach you, to illuminate your understanding, and show you how to apply God's Word. Quarreling about childish or elementary biblical things is proof of immaturity. I will only give my children greater responsibilities when I see they are mature enough to handle them. Maturity begets responsibility and obedience begets accountability, and as a parent, you must be sure not to give your child(ren) more responsibility than they're able to handle. Abba will not give great Kingdom responsibilities to immature sons. If you cannot rightly divide the Word of truth for yourself, how will you rightly divide the Word for someone else? If you are constantly ensnared and entangled in your own selfish ambitions, how will you free someone from the lusts of the world? Being led by the Spirit means being taught (not indoctrinated) by Holy Spirit. It means removing all preconceived knowledge about Christ and Christianity and allowing Holy Spirit to open your eyes to understand the scriptures from God's perspective and through His eyes. Abba is patient. He knows how much spiritual responsibility you are able to handle so please don't get ahead of Him.

    Mature sons are given weightier responsibilities in an effort to continue to train them as sons and eventual inheritors. Sons have distinct roles and positions within a family. Sons carry the name of their father and carry on the work of the father. Jesus came to fulfill the will of the Father (John 4:34) and that was His utmost desire and purpose for coming. Hebrews 5:8 says that although He was a Son, He learned obedience through His sufferings. In order for you to a become mature son, you too must submit to the Father's plan for your life and live in obedience to that plan, even in the face of personal suffering. God's family is the highest family in the universe and His Kingdom, the highest order. If the children of God grow into full maturity and become sons of God, they must understand how to legislate on behalf of Heaven. When you understand who we are, you understand that you have been sent here temporarily on assignment. As a son of God, you also receive governance or the right to advance the Kingdom of God by healing the sick, raising the dead, casting out demons, and so on. You have the Spirit of God living within you to carry out these marvelous exploits through Yeshua, our Messiah. You can speak a word of deliverance to someone who has been bound. You can trample on serpents and scorpions spiritually and not be harmed. You can ask according to the will of the Father, and it will be done for you. You can bind and loose according to God's will, and Heaven will back you. As a son of God, you have governing rights! So what are you doing with those rights?

      Mature sonship encompasses "discipline", and although this seems to be an ancient word these days, it is still required and vitally important to the believer today! This new life you are living is about endurance. It is about enduring persecution. It is about living a life in the Spirit and bringing to naught the works of the flesh. Hebrews 12:7 in the CJB says to regard your endurance as discipline for God is dealing with you as a son. He only chastens, disciplines and corrects those whom He loves. The verse goes on to say, "For what son goes undisciplined by his father? All legitimate sons undergo discipline; so if you don't, you're considered a mamzer and not a son!" (CJB) Wow! This verse is saying that sons are naturally disciplined by their fathers and this takes place out of love. We all should discipline our children because we love them. It is always for their good and not their detriment. God also chastens and disciplines His sons out of His love, and it is for your good and not your detriment. When you refuse the Lord's chastening, the verse says you are mamzer, which according to the online dictionary means, "Someone who is either born of adultery by a married Jewish woman and a Jewish man who is not her husband, or born of incest (as defined by the Bible), or someone who has a mamzer as a parent," (https://en.wikipedia.org/wiki/Mamzer). I don't know about you, but I don't want to be considered an illegitimate son because illegitimate sons have no inheritance rights! I want all of the benefits of being a true son, and in order to do that, I must be willing to be subject to God's loving correction, direction and discipline.

As mentioned throughout this chapter, you are a son, therefore an heir of God and joint-heir with Christ (Romans 8:17). This means that you, as a believer, have been allotted a possession by right of sonship. Paul reminds us in 2 Corinthians 1:22 that you and I have been sealed (for a security; from satan) with God's Spirit in our hearts as a guarantee (pledge or down payment) to confirm or attest to God's promise of inheritance. Salvation is just the beginning. Eternal life is not all we get. We get to experience the joys of sonship NOW! Inheritance gives you the right to act on your Father's behalf. In ancient times, sons were very careful not to misrepresent their fathers. Jesus was very careful not to do anything outside of the Father's will or to misrepresent Him. He was intentional about abandoning His own motives and agenda in order to fulfill the will of the Father.

Another striking reality is that sonship has all to do with birthright. The definition of birthright is a particular right of possession or privilege one has from birth, especially as an eldest child. Most of us know the story of Jacob and Esau in Genesis 25. After many years of barrenness, God opened Rebekah's womb, and she gave birth to two sons, Jacob and Esau. The two sons represented two nations who struggled from the womb and are still fighting today (I'll let you figure out who these two nations are). In verse 29, Jacob, the younger brother, cooked a stew, and Esau came in from the field famished and exhausted and asked Jacob to give him some of the red stew. Jacob, who's name means "heel holder; supplanter," told Esau that if he sold him his birthright, he could have the stew. Esau, obviously overwhelmed by his hunger and either negligent or ignorant of the benefits of his birthright, swore an oath to Jacob whereby selling his birthright to his younger brother. Under the law, the birthright went to the firstborn son and it included a double portion of the family estate (Nelson NKJ Study Bible), the right to represent his family (assume priestly duties), and the right to legislate on behalf of the family. Not only that, Jacob also inherited the everlasting covenant promises made by God through his forefathers. Jacob became legal heir by birthright. His name was later changed to Israel and he became father to the twelve tribes of Israel because he became legal holder of the birthright. Scripture declares that because you are a son, you too are an heir.

    Scripture tells us that believers are Abraham's seed and I have already elucidated about how we all have been grafted into the family/Kingdom of God (Galatians 3:29; Ephesians 3:6; Titus 3:7) upon our confession and belief. You are an inheritor of the promises made to Abraham, Isaac, Jacob and so on. You are legal a son because of the finished work of Jesus, and possessor of God's Kingdom by right of sonship. So what is your hindrance at this point? Failure to operate in your true identity will hinder, delay, or cause you to abort your divine assignment. It will render you powerless when the true tests come. Failure to walk in your true identity will cause spiritual blindness and apathy in spiritual things. Realized identity is the propeller to ruling and reigning. You can't rule as a king until you first know you are a king; then you must begin to function and live in that reality, as a king.

    I taught on this very topic during a trip to Moravian Falls and Holy Spirit led me to teach it during a mission's trip to Kumasi, Ghana in August of last year. The more I write and teach about it, the more confirmations I receive. I am convinced now more than ever that most Christians are not aware of their true identity or don't know how to live in their Kingdom identity. This requires more than just going to Bible study or Sunday services and gaining head knowledge. It is more than just reading your bible at home and praying. This is about coming into a Kingdom reality. It is knowing how to interact with Heaven and carrying out the work of Heaven. Is it about living out what Christ says about you. There are certain things you can only do if you have the legal right to do them. I cannot serve someone a search warrant if I am not a sheriff; I do not have the right authority or credentials. You have legal authority once you are a citizen of God's Kingdom. You have power over the enemy. Knowledge is half the battle. Walking in your authority is the other half. God the Father is supreme and has all authority over all, and we, through Jesus, are also given His authority. As an inheritor, you inherit what God has purposed for you. All of creation eagerly awaits the revealing of the sons of God (Romans 8:19), although it is currently undergoing the curse initially pronounced upon it due to the original sin. Abba's Spirit within you affirms that you belong to Him, but as you wait for the consummation of your sonship, you are to walk in the authority you have been granted thus far. There will be a great revealing of God's sons and all of creation will witness this. You are about to be put on display for all of Heaven and earth to see!

    In the story of the prodigal son, in exchange for his repentance and coming back, his father gave him a robe and signet ring signifying his new status. Although he was a son already, he wandered away and become lost to the grips of his internal passions and the unquenchable grip of the world. Once he came to himself and returned to his father's house, his sins (acts of rebellion) were forgiven. The father had compassion and changed his identity. He gave him back his position as son with much celebration. The Lord has done the same for you! Despite your dark past and rebellion against

Him, He had compassion, and through your repentance and faith, He has restored your identity and welcomed you into His glorious Kingdom. He exchanged your gloom for gladness and your weeping for His joy.

So, how do you begin to see yourself as a son? How do you begin to live your life as a son and legislate for the Kingdom of God? It begins with a renewed mind (Romans 12:1-2). About a year ago Holy Spirit led me to write an article about Baals, Scales and Veils. The article discussed the Baals we worship in our lives, the scales that keep us from seeing spiritually, and the veils we allow to cover our hearts and minds. Being a mature son means removing the scales, being healed of the veils, and tearing down and destroying the baals. There are many veils that can dull your understanding of God's Word and His ways. Religion can be a veil. It was a veil for the Pharisees and Sadducees that caused them to miss their long-awaited Messiah. While there are many things I can list as baals, scales and veils, the point is that you must begin with a renewed mind and heart in order to embrace the spiritual things of the Kingdom. You must allow your spirit (inner) man to rule and govern your soul and flesh man. Allow Holy Spirit to show you every veil and limitation so that you can walk in the liberty of the Spirit. Ask Jesus to anoint your eyes with eye salve (Revelation 3:18). How do you see spiritually? You see spiritually by knowing the Word and communing with the Word (Jesus). You also see spiritually by engaging the eyes of your heart by fixing them on Jesus. As you draw nigh to Him, He will begin to reveal things that you could not see or discern before. You have physical eyes and spiritual eyes so ask Holy Spirit to slowly show you how to see and discern from a spiritual perspective.

Hebrews 5:14 says that strong meat or solid food should be fed to those who are spiritually mature, to those who have trained their spiritual senses by continuous exercise to discern or distinguish between good and evil. Paul used this allegory to demonstrate the complexities of understanding God's Word. Here's an excellent saying from Charles Spurgeon about meat, "I have thus set before you the various sorts of strong meat. Before we leave the table let me utter a word of caution. Milk you may use as you will. You cannot take too much of it; it will not do strong men any great amount of good, but it will certainly do them no harm. But the strong meat must always be accompanied by a word of caution when it is placed before the uninstructed and feeble—since such are very apt to do mischief, both to themselves, and to others with this strong meat," (http://www.spurgeongems.org/vols7-9/chs506.pdf). Being a mature son has nothing to do with age and all to do with spiritual development. The more understanding you gain about God, the intricacies of His Word and how you should live, the more mature you become spiritually. And while some Christians may mature quicker than others, the goal should always be to move into maturity. Did you know that you have spiritual senses as well as physical senses? You have spiritual eyes that come into focus as you mature and exercise them. The Bible refers to your spiritual eyes as the eyes of your heart (Ephesians 1:18), and you use these eyes to see and discern spiritually. For those who walk in the office of a prophet or have the gift of prophecy or a seer, your spiritual eyes have been trained to see spiritual things.

    Living as a mature son requires fine-tuning your spiritual ears as well. Mature sons set out to hear the Father's gentle voice and will let nothing hinder their ability to hear the entreating voice of their King. Give him a map and a compass and set him in the middle of the desert and the mature believer will not move until He hears the voice of his beloved. Your eyes and ears must be calibrated to discern both good and the evil. Your nose must be familiar with the sweet fragrance of Jesus but also recognize the stench of evil. You must train your nostrils to recognize the wholesome and delicious smell of God's Word as well as detect the displeasing aroma of false doctrine, deceptive temptations and the like. You must also train your taste buds to know tasteless, watered-down misconceptions of truth. Psalm 34:8 says, "Oh taste and see that the LORD is good; Blessed is the man who trusts in Him!" Taste means "to perceive mentally," and see means "to perceive, have vision, distinguish and discern." In this passage, the psalmist asks the audience to use two spiritual (not physical) senses to perceive, discern and determine that the Lord is good. Lastly, we must also train our spiritual sense of touch. We must reach out and grab the hand of Jesus. You can wipe His feet with your tears and grab the hem of His garment. There have been times in worship when I have felt someone or some thing brush by me with such a gentle touch. The Lord desires to invite you into His secret place where you can experience Him in a very tangible way. Is this New Age? Absolutely not! Until last year, I had never heard of such a thing. My teacher has been Holy Spirit and I have so enjoyed this journey of discovery. I love where Abba takes our team in worship and none of us could do what we do without an authentic relationship with the Lord and understanding the principles of His Kingdom.

 Because you are a son, you get the awesome privilege to commune with the Lord at anytime. You get to enjoy a beautiful friendship with Jesus that the world is totally oblivious to. You get to hear His voice and discern His heart. You get the awesome opportunity to be "wooed" by Holy Spirit and made to feel His love and compassion for you. You get to walk through life with the Creator, your hand in His hand, and your head upon His heart. You get to hear His plans for His creation and His people. How priceless a gift we share! Worship is no longer a song, but a life you live. Sonship is your right. Jesus died to give you sonship. You are an heir. You have an inheritance. Change the way you see yourself. Put on your new identity. You are a son of God! By faith, begin to live in this Kingdom reality. You are no longer a slave but a son. You have been adopted into the Beloved. Challenge and change the way you currently see yourself. Pray daily and ask Holy Spirit to guide you in your assignment as a son. Take authority over your family, finances, churches, children, marketplaces, and governments and refuse to allow the enemy possession of what rightfully belongs to you. Ask Holy Spirit to open your spiritual eyes and unveil who you really are to Him. You have a destiny to fulfill. You have purpose to accomplish. Yes, Jesus will complete the good work He has begun in you, but you must start moving. Put your hands to the plow and let nothing stop you. You are a son of royalty. Your Father rules and He is waiting for you to navigate your course of life in your role as His son.

CHAPTER SIX

Kings and Priests of God

"To Him who loved us and washed us from our sins in His own blood, and has made us kings and priests to His God and Father, to Him be glory and dominion forever and ever. Amen."
Revelation 1:5b-6

"But you are a chosen generation, a royal priesthood, a holy nation, His own special people, that you may proclaim the praises of Him who called you out of darkness into His marvelous light; who once were not a people but are now the people of God, who had not obtained mercy but now have obtained mercy."
1 Peter 2:9-10

In this chapter, we will delve into the precepts of what it means to be a king and priest of God. To be honest, this entire book was written based upon one prevailing revelatory truth the Lord spoke to me regarding authority. I shared earlier that while I was seeking Holy Spirit for a specific need, He said, "You are a king and priest in my Kingdom; walk as such in the earth." That one revelatory statement set me on a path to unveil what it meant to walk as a king and priest here on earth. This truth also regrettably revealed to me that obviously I was not walking in my kingly and priestly roles, so this chapter will be a chapter of deeper discovery. With this deeper understanding of king and priest came a new insight. I would no longer see myself the same. I would no longer pray the same. I would no longer approach God's throne in the same way, and I hope this same profound truth will radically transform your life and perspective forever.

In the previous chapter, I discussed in detail how you, through Christ, have been declared a son of God. You now understand that sonship is just one component of your identity in Christ. God's covenantal promises belong to all who will embrace their sonship and walk in maturity and freedom. You also understand that sonship has to do with inheritance rights and because of this knowledge, you will no longer approach the Father as a slave, but as a legally, adopted son from a royal and kingly order. You know that Jesus is the eternal Son of God and His inheritance will result in universal dominion, and because He will rule over everyone and everything both now and forever, you will share in this dominion and ruler-ship. You are a son and Jesus is THE Son, and we all have one Father (Hebrews 2:12). All who have been truly born again have become manifested sons who interact with God's Kingdom. You must leave the mindset of the world behind and transform your life after the One you belong to.

Revelation 1:5b-6 explains that Jesus loved us and washed us from our sins in His own blood and because of this atoning act, we are now kings and priests to His Father. The Greek word for kings is **basileus and it means,** "leader of the people, prince, commander, lord of the land, king." There are other Bible translations that use the word basileia, which means "kingdom," and translates this verse to say we have been made a Kingdom of priests to our God but the correct transliteration is basileus.

What we will dissect in this chapter is how Christ became both High Priest and King, which according to Jewish tradition and history, had never been accomplished before except by Melchizedek. Melchizedek is first mentioned in Genesis 14 and identified during that time as the king of Salem, also known as Jerusalem. He was not only king but also priest of God Most High (Genesis 14:18), and many believe he was the preincarnate Son of God. Melchizedek served as both king and priest.

Your Identity in Christ

According to Psalm 24:1, everything belongs to God and He has given total ruler-ship to Christ. Jesus has given you both power and position to rule with Him and represent Heaven (I can't say this enough). Psalm 115:16 declares, "The Heaven, even the Heavens, are the LORD'S; But the earth He has given to the children of men." We have been given authority to rule and govern the earth. Kings rule and priests serve. Now I know some of you may be wondering how to function in all of these various roles and I will explain that. Some also may be wondering how can you rule in today's organized democracy. Let me ask you this. Do you know when to function as a manager on your job? Does anyone have to tell you? Do you know when, where and how to function as a mother or father or teacher or counselor or coach? No, your surroundings, location, and audience dictate the role you should assume. When I'm at home, I'm in the role of a mother and wife. When I'm at work, I step into my designated work role. When I'm at church, I step into my designated ministry role. What happens when you step into a role at the wrong place or at the wrong time? You operate outside of your designated authority. There will be times when you pray as a son of God. There will be times when the devil is on your trail and you must step into your role as king and declare victory over your situation and defeat the one attempting to destroy you. There will be times when you step into your priestly role and offer up intercessions for the lost, the weak, the sick, etc. The emphasis I am making here is that you should know what role to operate in at any given time and when to step into that role or position of authority. Kings and priests are spiritual identities and you must know how and when to operate in them according to the leading of Holy Spirit.

Now I know there may be some who feel that your ultimate ruler-ship will not take place until you are actually reigning alongside Christ in Heaven, but here's my opinion. There are areas of your life where you can begin to rule and reign right now. How you ask? Let's look at Matthew 18:18. Jesus tells His disciples, "Assuredly, I say to you, whatever you bind on earth will be bound in Heaven, and whatever you loose on earth will be loosed in Heaven." The word bind in this passage is the Greek word "deo" and it means, "to forbid, prohibit, to declare illicit." Binding and loosing were common terms among the Jewish culture where one was allowed to declare something lawful or unlawful, legal or illegal. There is a position of kingly authority that you possess which allows you to declare things unlawful or lawful in the realm of the spirit, according to the Word and will of the Father. If something is contrary to the Word of God, you can declare it illegal and so will Heaven. For example, if you are experiencing pain, you have the right to pray and declare that particular pain illegal in your body. There is no sickness in Christ and you can claim your covenant promise of health and healing by taking your position as a king and son and by releasing a decree through binding. Christ will ratify what is done in His name on earth as long as it is in alignment with His sovereign will. Whatever you bind here on earth will be bound in Heaven and the same goes with loosing. You can declare sickness illegal and loose healing. I must also say this, just because you may feel a little pain after your prayers, please do not allow doubt and unbelief to counter your binding. Although this is taking the position of a spiritual king and exercising your heavenly authority, it must be done by faith. Faith is what causes Heaven to respond, so everything we do, pray and say must be released from a place of victory and faith.

    Again, how do you step into your identity as king for Christ? In the Kingdom, thoughts are creative and have astronomical power. When you read the Word of God, you must do more than just read it, you must internalize it. The revelation of the Word must become truth and when you embrace it as truth, you must begin to live out the reality of that truth. Faith has everything to do with what and how you think and respond. Do you believe God's Word? Do you believe He is working on your behalf? It's not enough for me to tell you that you are a son, a king, and a priest; you must accept the revealed Word as truth, believe it, start to see yourself as a son, priest and king, and apply this truth to your everyday life. For example, if I see myself as worthless, repugnant and apathetic, then my countenance, speech and viewpoint in life will be centered on how I see myself. On the contrary, if I see myself as confident, beautiful and productive, then my behavior will exemplify the thoughts I hold as truth. If you embrace the fact that you are so loved that God appointed you a son in His Kingdom and a king, and you begin to walk in this reality by praying from the place of sonship, then everything around you will change because of your new perspective. When you change the way you think about yourself, you will begin to see your circumstances differently. When you begin to see yourself as God sees you, your approach to life's circumstances will change tremendously. By changing your perception, you will begin to live life differently. You have been called to live the ascended life. It's a higher life with greater rewards.

Speaking of disposition, did you know that the thoughts you think will either attract dark energy (spirits) or light energy (Heaven's designee's)? Regarding Kingdom principles, did you know that when you think negative, faithless, jealous, evil, negative thoughts that you attract the kingdom of darkness, and when you think positive, peaceful, faith-filled, godly, pure thoughts, you attract the Kingdom of light? When your thoughts align with God's Holy Word, you have the interaction of Heaven via angels. The Father sees your thoughts and will respond to them when you operate from a place of songship and kingship. Without saying a word, the Father knows your every thought (Psalm 94:11).

Let's talk about kingship. Christ came through the line of David and the tribe of Judah. The Gospels of Matthew and Luke outline the genealogy and origin of Jesus in order to prove His inheritable authenticity to the Jews; to prove that He was their long-awaited Messiah. Because genealogy was important and required in order to authenticate a person's lineal legitimacy and eligibility, it was important for the religious sects of Jesus' day to know that Jesus was qualified to be king. Matthew traced Jesus' genealogy back to Abraham, thus proving that He was indeed an Israelite and also through David to prove that Jesus was from the kingly line and qualified to rule on David's throne. Luke traced Jesus' genealogy through Mary all the way back to Adam. Psalm 2:6 in the NLT states, "For the Lord declares, 'I have placed my chosen king on the throne in Jerusalem, on my holy mountain.'" Although God allowed earthly kings to rule over His people, He has set His Son as the one and only legitimate King of kings who is now seated on the throne in the Heavens. Jesus was the king of the Jews but they did not recognize Him as king because they were looking for external kingly qualities and a governmental ruler who would eliminate their Roman oppression. Instead, Jesus came as a humble servant confounding the very perception of what a king should be. Jesus was in line to be Israel's next king, and in fact, He was their rightful king and the genealogies prove it. Even the wise men were smart enough to know that He was king. They followed His star and found Him and offered gifts that only someone of a royal lineage would receive (Matthew 2). Just as Jesus received gifts fit for a king, you too have been promised crowns for the work you will complete on earth which signify kingly rule and authority. The crowns are the: Crown of Rejoicing, Crown of

Righteousness, Crown of Life, Crown of Glory and the Incorruptible Crown. Revelation 4 gives a prolific imagery of what you should do with these crowns when you receive them; you should cast them at the feet of Jesus!

Today, Israel is not ruled or governed by a king by way of monarchy, but she has a royal, eternal King who is enthroned in Heaven. We know that according to Revelation 17:17 and 19:16, Jesus is the King of Kings. He will reign over all the kingdoms of the earth and the body of Christ will rule with Him. His throne will last forever and His scepter is a scepter of righteousness and justice (Psalm 45:6). Being a king deals with governance and authority. Psalm 2:7 speaks of the Messiah's triumph and and the King's ability to declare the decree of the Father. Everything God does is by His decrees and according to His sovereign will. As a king, you can release the decree or Word of the Lord over your various nations, families, communities, and governments and impact change. According to The Nelson Study Bible, every time a legitimate son of David was crowned a successor, the new king was adopted by God as His son. A coronation was held that encompassed high, exuberant praise and included the priests and prophets to affirm this adoption.

Jesus is the eternal successor of David and is seated on the heavenly throne, begotten of God the Father as His one true Son. You are to rule in your respective spheres of influence whereby you bring earthly things into alignment with Heaven. God wants His Kingdom to come on earth as it is in Heaven and you are the human vehicle appointed to decree such an alignment. When you speak the words of Jesus with authority, you begin to set things in motion for His Kingdom to come and rule. You can see governments and cities change if you pray from a place of kingship.

Veronica Evans

In the past several years, I have seen a tremendous decrease of prayer in the church. Our services are filled with flamboyant praise, liturgical dancers, mimers, state-of-the-art media announcements and events that jam-pack our church services, but I see very little prayer taking place (I'm not knocking any of these; I'm just pointing out priorities). In Matthew 21:13, Jesus emphatically states that His house shall be called a house of prayer. Our physical churches and our bodily temples should be houses of intense prayer. You will not change governments and communities and families if you, as the church, are not praying. If you want to go deeper in the things of God, be earnest about your prayer time with Jesus. If you want to see your loved ones saved, be consistent in praying for them. If you want your church to fulfill the call of God, spend more time in prayer rather than in entertaining events. The disciples and followers of Jesus were in prayer when Holy Spirit came as a mighty rushing wind (Acts 2:2). It was at midnight that Paul and Silas prayed and sang psalms and an angel came and shook the foundation of the prison where they were being held and opened the prison doors (Acts 16:25). When the disciples tried to cast out a demon and were unsuccessful, Jesus told them that some demonic strongholds will only come forth by fasting and prayer (Mark 9:29). What am I trying to say? The authority that Jesus died to give you and me can only be cultivated through a life of prayer, faith, spiritual discipline, and an all-out devotion to our Savior. When believers fail to walk in the fullness of his/her authority and identity, they diminish the power of Christ in their lives. The world is watching the church. They want to see this God she so bodaciously brags about. Signs and wonders will follow those who know how to pray as sons and kings of God.

The word "priest" is the Greek word hiereus and the Hebrew word cohanim and means "one who offers sacrifices or sacred rites." According to the Blueletter Bible, the word priest is a metaphor for "Christians because, purified by the blood of Christ and brought into close intercourse with God, they devote their life to him alone and to Christ." Because you have been appointed as a Kingdom priest, you have been given the awesome privilege of offering spiritual sacrifices to your King and you no longer have to wait for another priest to go before God on your behalf. The veil has been torn forever and it is not God's intention for man to resurrect the veil again. You can now enter the Holy of Holies and offer spiritual sacrifices as a priest.

In the Old Testament, the priesthood was reserved for the tribe of Levi, the sons of Aaron (Deuteronomy 10:8). They were designed by God to carry the Ark of the Covenant, to stand before Him, to minister to Him and to bless His name. The High Priest was the only priest permitted to enter the Holy of Holies once a year to offer animal sacrifices for himself and on behalf of the people. This priesthood was only extended through bloodline; one had to be born into the lineage of Levi in order to be a part of the priestly line. Oh, but this is where the work of the cross has changed everything for you and me. Paul extrapolated in great detail the new priesthood order to which new covenant believers belong. Abba Father says in Psalm 110:4, "The Lord has sworn And will not relent, 'You are a priest forever According to the order of Melchizedek.'" Paul also quoted this verse in Hebrews 5:6 to affirm the changing of the Levitical priesthood from an earthly, temporal priesthood to a spiritual, eternal priesthood. God the Father swore and will not relent that Jesus IS priest forever after the pattern or rank of Melchizedek, and this order can never change again.

When Jesus came, all of the Old Testament types and shadows were fulfilled in and through Him. As so many have quoted over the years, "The Old Testament is Christ concealed and the New Testament is Christ revealed." Hebrews chapter 5 tells of the qualifications of a priest. A priest had to be one called by God, could identify with human nature, and would represent man to God. The high priest would offer gifts and sacrifices for sins on the altar on behalf of himself and the people, especially on the Day of Atonement.

      God appointed Aaron as priest. Jesus Christ did not descend through the line of Levi; however, we see in Psalm 110 and Hebrews 5:6 that God the Father appointed Christ a Priest forever according to or like the priesthood of Melchizedek. The entire book of Hebrews proclaims the superiority of Jesus Christ. Paul set out to prove that Jesus was greater in superiority than the angels, Moses, Joshua, the Hebrew High Priests, and that Christ made a better sacrifice established upon better promises. Jesus eradicated the old priesthood by rendering it obsolete, and through faith in Him, He has created a new and living way. His atoning blood sealed the deal for you and me. The book of Hebrews solidifies the fact that Jesus is superior in His person, superior in His sacrificial work, and that faith, rather than works, is the better way.

      In order to understand who you are as a priest, you must first understand Jesus' role and position as your High Priest. The Old Testament requirements of priesthood have been eliminated for now, and Abba has instituted a new priesthood order according to the rank of Melchizedek, not Levi. One of the main requirements of a priest was he had to be able to relate to the people or identify with their human nature. Jesus fulfilled this requirement according to Hebrews 4:14-15, "Seeing then that we have a great High Priest who has passed through the Heavens, Jesus the Son of God, let us hold fast our confession. For we do not have a High Priest who cannot sympathize with our weaknesses, but was in all points tempted as we are, yet without sin." Isn't that wonderful to know? There is nothing you and I will go through in life that Jesus cannot identify with. He was tempted just as you are. He was persecuted just as you are. He had to obey just as you do. The theme of the book of Hebrews is "Christ is better." Jesus is better than the Old Testament priests with all of the sacrifices and ceremonial requirements. The Old Testament ways could not save humanity and offer them the peace and freedom Jesus secured. The Jews were considering returning to the old ways of Judaism, but Paul was set out to prove his assertion by declaring that the ways of Christ were better and higher than the customs they had left behind. He emphasized that going back to Judaism would prove detrimental to their spiritual growth.

Genesis 14 records Abraham's encounter with Melchizedek. Melchizedek was the King of Salem (Jerusalem) and priest of God Most High (El Elyon). His name means, "My King is Righteous" or "King of Righteousness". This Melchizedek was very mystical in that he had no lineage, no mention of mother or father and he was an extreme resemblance of the Son of God. Abba has appointed Jesus as both King and Priest just as Melchizadek was priest and king, something totally prohibited in Old Testament Jewish culture.

King Uzziah had to pay a hefty price for overstepping his boundaries and authority by attempting to exalt himself as a priest (2 Chronicles 26:16-23). The office of priest and king could not be combined; however, God called Jesus to be priest and king without interruption, without successor and forever. Melchizedek met Abraham after he had recovered Lot, his family and his goods from captivity. (Let me also mention that the encounter with Abraham and Melchizedek is the first mention of tithing, making it a precedent for the Old Testament law of tithing). As a New Testament believer, you fall under the Melchizedek order of tithing and not that of the Levitical order, so to reference the scriptures of Malachi as a basis for the tithe would be addressing the wrong priesthood order. Melchizedek blessed Abraham and gave him bread and wine, and in return Abraham gave him a tithe of all the possessions he had collected. It is very apparent that because Abraham gave Melchizedek a tithe, he considered him a priest, as well as king because tithes were only given to the priests.

Jesus has been appointed as High Priest, not according to human lineage or ancestry, but according to the power of an endless life (Hebrews 7:15-16). There has been a change in the priesthood. The Levitical priesthood was mortal, whereby men died and had to be replaced; however, the priesthood of Melchizedek is an eternal priesthood with an unchangeable High Priest. The requirement of the High Priest was to offer sacrifices. Jesus met all of the requirements of a priest because of the finished work of the Cross. He offered Himself as the perfect sacrifice once and for all.

If you are a royal priesthood, a chosen generation, a holy nation, how do you live in this reality? How do you conduct yourself as a priest of the Most High? What do you do as a priest of God? Hebrews 7:25 says that Jesus lives to make intercession for us and His priesthood is no longer transferrable, meaning there's no other human bloodline to inherit His royal priesthood. In the Old Testament, as priests died, their offices were transferred to the next priest in line. Old Testament priests offered sacrifices, and we too can offer spiritual sacrifices to Christ with the fruit of our lips, giving praise to God continually (Heb. 13:15). When you share with others, this is also accounted as a sacrifice in which God is well pleased (Hebrews 13:16). When you come before God's holy throne of grace in prayer, you can pray from a position of a priest, but you must see yourself as priests of God where you can legally appear before Him to serve and worship Him. As a New Testament believer, you are under a new priesthood order where you have been given the divine authority to operate as Abba's priest. Your new bloodline has qualified you. In the Old Testament, the Holy of Holies separated man from God, but now the veil has been torn and we, God's serving priests, can enter behind the veil and worship Him before His throne. As you light the candles of incense, which represent your prayers and worship, you must do so with a humble heart. As a priest, you are to take the shewbread or the bread of His presence, which represents His Word, and eat it, for it is manna to your spirit. As a priest, you must allow the light (golden candlestick) and Presence of Holy Spirit to infiltrate your heart and inner being until you become transformed into His very image.

When you are able to approach the throne of grace wearing Jesus' robe of righteousness, you will find answers to your problems. It is when you come before the presence of God that you find rest in times of difficulty, secure wisdom to make sound judgments and decisions, and receive healing for your mind, body and your soul. As a priest, you get the opportunity to minister to the Lord. You get to bring your gifts to Him and hear His heart on various matters. You get to hear the sweet sound of His voice and encounter His indescribable glory. Can you really experience all this? Absolutely! The Lord wants to commune with you. He is not some distant, intolerant God who wants nothing to do with His creation. The Bible says that God is love, and since love is not love until it is given away, He wants you to know what true, agape love looks and feels like.

Jesus is waiting for you to step into your role as priests, and cry out for your nation, family, community, and government. By fervently interceding in these areas, you allow your prayers to make way for Heaven's intervention and Heaven's mediation. You have the capacity within you to change your environment. You carry a vibration within you capable of shifting any atmosphere. You can change the current situation you're in by changing your perspective of who you are, standing in your true identity, and releasing prayers and decrees according to God's prophetic Word. Old Testament priests served God day and night in His Temple, and you can do the same by always being present with God and listening for the voice of Holy Spirit.

    As I am continuing to learn how to function in my Kingdom identity, I am witnessing a radical change in my prayer life. I am witnessing quick answers to prayers and experiencing deeper intimacy with Jesus. God always sees things and people in their completed forms. I no longer see myself as a victim, an outcast, a sinner, powerless, a rebel, a transgressor, an enemy, intimidated, or a fornicator. Now that my former life has died in Christ, I choose to see myself through the eyes of Jesus as a warrior bride, a mature son, a king, a priest, a victor, an ambassador, and a friend of God. I choose to see myself this way. It is an act of my will. I refuse to allow my mind to cause me to think contrary. If the Bible says I am a son, then I am a son with inherited rights.

    If the Bible says you are a king, then you are a king who can rule and govern for Heaven with authority. If the Bible says you are a priest, then you are a priest who can go before the Father and offer spiritual sacrifices and intercession to Him. If the Bible says it, then that settles it!

    Satan is the master deceiver and he wants nothing more than for you to live outside of your true identity. As a matter of fact, he would love to offer you a counterfeit or false identity. It's time for you to get up, put on your priestly garments, and make an appearance before Jesus. Jesus has removed your filthy garments and has given you a robe of righteousness, so put it on with confidence. Go before the Father in reverent prayer. Let Holy Spirit take you beyond the corridors of time and into His timeless presence. You have the word of deliverance for someone's life. What are you praying? Release your fragrant incense before the Lord as His king and priest and look for things to change.

God appointed Jesus Christ as High Priest forever and He sits on a throne. He reigns and so do you! When you are able to understand these truths and walk in them, you liken yourself to a wise man who built his/her house upon a rock. In the days and months ahead, you will be challenged with walking in your true Kingdom identity. As the world becomes more intolerant of Christianity, only your spiritual position and identity will help you navigate the path of righteousness. Knowledge, socioeconomic status, and religious affiliation will not bring you comfort and peace in this very chaotic world. You will have to KNOW Christ and be known by Him. You will have to KNOW who you are in the Kingdom of God and refuse to digress from the Word of God and Christianity as a whole. Set your will now. Move into full maturity where you can move forward in the "rest" of God (Hebrews 4:9). Your victory will not come through power, nor by might, but by God's Spirit leading you, so remain anchored in Him and walk in your true identity as a king and priest.

CHAPTER SEVEN

Kingdom Ambassadors

"Now then, we are ambassadors for Christ, as though God were pleading through us: we implore you on Christ's behalf, be reconciled to God"
2 Corinthians 5:20

The final role I will discuss is that of an ambassador. When I think of an ambassador, I think of someone with governmental authority who represents a certain king, nation, and/or government. By definition an ambassador is someone who lives in one country but represents his/her home country in/from another nation or country. From a Kingdom perspective, ambassadors are representatives of the Sovereign who sent them.

You know that you belong to the Kingdom of God. The Kingdom of God is within you (Luke 17:21) as well as around you. You carry the fragrance and authority of the Kingdom. You have been called by your King to serve as His ambassadors on earth, in a world that is in extreme rebellion against the Lord Jesus Christ.

A Kingdom ambassador serves as God's agent in the earth, and because he is a foreigner in his assigned territory, he does not entangle himself with the governmental affairs of the nation or country in which he/she lives. An ambassador can also be called a "consulate" and can be a person of high rank who has been given the indelible right to represent his own government or sovereign in an assigned location for a set amount of time. In the host country, the ambassador oversees the safety of citizens in foreign countries. One thing he/she has to be extremely careful about is how he/she governs affairs in the designated foreign country. An ambassador does not offend the host nation in any manner or bring disrepute upon his home country. Wisdom is a precious commodity for an ambassador.

As an ambassador of the Lord Jesus Christ, you must not embrace the governmental views of this world that are contrary to the Word of God (I am not advocating breaking any laws). If the very essence of God is life, then we cannot embrace and support anything that honors and supports murder or death on any level. Ambassadors in the Bible were considered "presbeuo" or elders and were people with great wisdom and maturity, as well as individuals who were older in age. An ambassador could never be viewed as a novice.

So how do you walk as Christ's ambassador? What do you say on behalf of the Heavenly Kingdom? Paul said we are to speak for Christ and plead to unbelievers, "Come back to God." It is God who speaks through you as you make an appeal to mankind. And, just what is your message you ask? Reconciliation! When you speak and move on His behalf, it is Jesus walking and speaking and moving through you. Because you are "in" Him, His words released from your mouth and mixed with your faith, have tremendous life and power. God wants to speak and release His plan for humanity through you. He wants to give you influence and favor to appeal to man's hearts on His behalf. Paul said we are to implore mankind to be reconciled back to God. What Adam and Eve lost in the Garden, Jesus restored at Calvary. You are no longer an alien and enemy of God but His representative. When you preach or teach and make known the way of the cross, you are making an appeal and acting on behalf of Heaven. 2 Peter 3:9 states, "The Lord is not slack concerning His (emphasis added) promise, as some count slackness, but is longsuffering toward us, not willing that any should perish but that all should come to repentance." It is Jesus' utmost desire that none of mankind be lost or perish. He wants all to live the abundant life that He offers, but He leaves the choice to choose this life to each and every individual. Jesus paved the way to a rightful relationship with the Father through the shedding of His precious blood. Confession and belief in His name (Romans 10:9) are the entry points to reconciliation. You have been sent forth to point the world to a better way of life through the higher Kingdom order of Jesus the Messiah.

An ambassador understands his/her rights and authority. His/Her credentials have already been established and their ordainment has already been predestined. He/She is a diplomat who understands how to govern his/her country's affairs. He/She understands the tremendous responsibility he/she carries. He/She understands that he/she has been approved and sent on behalf of his/her country on a temporary basis. Most importantly, an ambassador fully understands that he/she is not living within the host country to give his/her own opinion or to accomplish his/her own personal agenda. Rather, his/her ultimate goal is to advance the agenda of his/her own king. He/She is faithful to the task, hospitable to the host nation and comforts and guides the people who are from the same homeland.

Just as I explained in the previous chapters, this road to discovering your identity in Christ has everything to do with renewing your mind. Identity has everything to do with self- perception and self-awareness…how you see yourself. You must put on the mind of Christ. You must remove the false identities placed upon you by yourself, the enemy, your culture, your family, and so on. You must wrap your mind around the fact that God designed you uniquely and has an awesome purpose for you. God sees you complete although you're still going through the maturation process. Jeremiah complained to God because he was young and could not speak but Jeremiah failed to realize that people cannot highlight their "deficiencies" to the One who created them (Jeremiah 1:6). God knew what Jeremiah could and could not do because He meticulously designed him. The Lord told Jeremiah not to say that he was young or to dwell on his inadequacies because his destiny had already been sealed. So while Jeremiah was looking at his present self and present condition, and might I add seeing himself through immature eyes, the Lord was telling him He had been ordained a prophet to the nations (verse 10). Jeremiah saw himself in the present but God saw him in his fullness!

Ah! You cannot look at yourself in the natural. You need to see your spiritual self. There are gifts and abilities locked inside of you waiting to be released. You need to ask Holy Spirit to change the lens on your scope. Don't let the real you lie dormant! In this next season it is paramount that you discover your true Kingdom identity. We, as a nation, have entered a time where man's identity is being challenged on every side. Jeremiah was given a series of visions in order to heighten his perceptibility and vision for the things of God. What he saw with his eyes was interpreted by God to ensure Jeremiah understood the revelation of what he was seeing. Ah ha! Herein lies the problem with vision and perceptibility! Holy Spirit must interpret visions from God in order to provide understanding and knowledge of greater truths. You cannot always rely on people to interpret things for you. There has to be revelation and understanding of truth in order to rightly engage and embrace the truths presented. Summarily, just knowing who you are biologically does not provide the revelation of who you are in God's Kingdom, although it does play a part. As a matter of fact, some of us come from such dysfunctional homes and families that knowing who you are in God is quite liberating. Your biological identity is important but you are never limited by it. You have been grafted into a spiritual family and you posses a higher, spiritual identity.

If there's one thing I have learned on my journey with the Lord, it is that of interpretation and revelation. It's very interesting that I have heard many preachers say that there is no new revelation. I don't altogether agree with that statement because anything that you did not know or fully understand prior to revelation or illumination, for that matter, is new—even if only to you. There are many scriptures I have read over the years, but it was not until Holy Spirit illuminated or revealed the spiritual meaning to that particular scripture that I could understand it and walk in it. It's like when Jesus told Nicodemus that in order to see the Kingdom of God, a man must be born again. Nicodemus, in his finite understanding, attempted to equate this birth to a physical new birth but knew a physical rebirth was highly impossible. He was attempting to understand spiritual things through logic and reasoning. Jesus always taught from a spiritual perspective and even the disciples had difficulty understanding the majority of the spiritual truths He taught. The new birth Jesus referenced to Nicodemus dealtt with a spiritual new birth and in order to function in a Kingdom reality, you must seek to understand spiritual things. Yes, you must set out to study to show yourself approved to God by rightly dividing the word of truth (2 Timothy 2:15). And, as you study the Word, you must ask Holy Spirit to speak in order to open your spiritual eyes and ears to the Kingdom meaning of the Word or else you will try to understand it with a very carnal mindset. Discernment will be key in this hour so pray for it and receive it by faith.

Ambassadors are faithful and true to their mission and you too must remain faithful to the mission. I lead a ministry and at any given time, I am confident that I could send one of my team members to a particular place to represent the ministry and they would do it well. Any member of the team can represent the ministry unconditionally and with a spirit of excellence because of the time we have spent together. They understand the ministry's mission and goals. They know me as an individual. They know how I think and how I operate. They are clearly trustworthy enough to carry out a meeting and/or rehearsal the way they know I would. Would they deviate from what they know I would want? No. Why? Because they understand the mission, the focus and the goal of the ministry and they are true to the mission. Only a person who is immature or who has a different agenda would set out to do something totally opposite of the mission at hand.

Jesus was focused and strategic about His mission. He even spoke directly to Peter and said, "Get thee behind me, Satan: thou art an offence unto me: for thou savourest not the things that be of God, but those that be of men," (Matthew 16:23-KJV). Did you get what Jesus was really saying to Peter? Jesus instantly recognized that satan attempted to use Peter to distract Him from His mission. He charged satan and Peter with seeing things from a carnal perspective. Although Peter was undeniably ripped to the core at the very thought of Jesus dying so soon, his heroic attempt to save Him proved detrimental to the plan of God.

What does this mean for you? When the Lord reveals the purpose for which you are created, you cannot let anyone, and I do mean anyone, distract you from fulfilling your Kingdom assignment. There are many of you reading this book whom God will give a sphere of influence to counsel and minster to governmental leaders, pastors, city and state officials, and the like, but you cannot allow their opinions to derail you. While there are many in the church that would like to offer you super spiritual advice, make sure it is godly counsel. Satan will use anyone, even those closest to you, to try to get you off course. Because your family members have such a strong tie to you, they my at times see things carnally because they are concerned more about your physical safety or your reputation. You must stay true to your spiritual assignment despite family members who may not understand your Kingdom destiny.

As a mature ambassador, you will be called to speak on behalf of the Kingdom. Whether it's to a co-worker or a senator, you are Christ's representative. Will your words be full of faith? Will they be in the power, love and in the demonstration of Holy Spirit? Will you be able to stand against the opposing threats of non-spiritual people and declare what thus saith the Lord? Paul said that you are an ambassador of Christ, that God is making His appeal through you. How will you appeal on behalf of Heaven?

When you know what you have been designed and created to do, there is an inner strength that you draw from. Holy Spirit is your confidence and He lets you know constantly that it is He who works through you. He reassures you that you are on the right path and as long as you follow Him, you are destined for great things. This journey of discovering your identity in Christ is exhilarating and will saturate you in Jesus' love and strength. Do you have to look like an ambassador from the world's perspective to be one? Do you have to dress like an ambassador to be one? No! In the eyes of the Jewish people of Jesus' day, Jesus did not look like a king but He was one. From their perspective, He didn't look like the Messiah, but He was the Messiah! They expected the Messiah to come and rule as King, not to take the position of a suffering servant and die on a rugged cross. You are an ambassador in the Heavenly Kingdom even if you don't look the part. The sooner you acknowledge who you are to the Lord, the sooner you walk in a holy boldness like never before. The Father wants your life journey to be exciting. He wants to take you on the adventure of your life. He has treasures waiting for you to discover and your identity in Christ is just one of them! Release yourself from your old mindset that has no idea of who you really are in Christ. You must agree that you are an ambassador then see yourself as an ambassador. You are an authoritative agent of Heaven!

Another striking characteristic of an ambassador is his/her ability to avoid misrepresentation of his/her nation and/or sovereign. He/She has to be very gentle and wise in business affairs with the host nation. He/She must continue to follow the laws, customs, and traditions of his/her own country, though he/she may be contrastingly different from his/her host country. If America is your host nation and you are here as an ambassador, you have an obligation to convey the message of your Sovereign to your people in that land and stay true to the culture of your homeland. Similarly your citizenship is in Heaven; therefore, you must embrace the laws (His word), traditions and customs of the Kingdom of God. The sooner you embrace the fact that you are not in this world to stay, the sooner you can move forward with the mission of Christ, even if it costs you hardship, imprisonment, isolation, or misunderstanding.

Jesus was mocked, ridiculed, misunderstood, falsely accused, beaten, and imprisoned. Yet He remained faithful to the agenda of His Father unto death. In fulfilling the role of an ambassador, He was sent to earth on behalf of Heaven to represent Heaven. He did not conform to the traditions and religions of man. He came to present a new, living way of the Father. And as you read the Gospels, from the introduction to their close, Jesus reminded the disciples and the people that a new Kingdom order was among them. He was sent to declare and demonstrate that the Kingdom of God had arrived.

So let me ask you, what kingdom legacy will you leave behind? Will you be someone known for your tenacious faith and your undaunting and unwavering stand for truth? You have a designated path to navigate. You have people waiting to hear your appeal. You will be given an opportunity to represent your King. You will be given a chance to demonstrate the traditions of your homeland. You must KNOW your King and how He wants you to represent Him. Take Esther for example. This beautiful orphan, the fairest in the land of Persia, was chosen for an appointed time. She had one time to get it right with the king. It was what she was born and positioned for, and once she came into that reality, she moved forward in the plan and purpose of God for His people. She risked her own life to save the lives of her people. This authority, to do or say something on behalf of the Lord, is not about you. It is about fulfilling the will of the Lord through you. The Father has chosen you to partner in His plan for humanity and you must consider it an honor. Anytime the King invites you to join Him in His plan, it is indeed an honor. Your allegiance is not to a flag but to your Almighty God. So rise up, Esthers! Rise up, Davids and Jeremiahs and Joshuas! Rise up, Sarahs and Marys and Rachels. You are mighty in the Kingdom of God. Go and tell those in your sphere of influence about the Good News of the Gospel of the Kingdom. You don't have to be a Pastor or Evangelist. God is sending you forth as His agent so arise and walk in your ambassadorial identity!

  Ambassadors must willingly submit to the Lordship of their king. There is never a question as to who's in charge. An ambassador never has to worry about what to say because he follows the orders of his king. As an ambassador, you must say what the Word says. And, as an ambassador, you have the authority to cast down and immediately destroy any word that is contrary to the Word of the Lord..

Ambassadors can be trusted with the smallest of tasks. They are dependable and reliable and experts at paying attention to detail. They do not seek accolades or recognition or status or titles or such. Because they have the credentials to be an ambassador, they are content to function in that role wholeheartedly.

As the Lord's agents in the earth, you must pray continually for eyes to see and ears to hear. Because you represent the Kingdom, you have the grave responsibility of making sure you are operating in both a physical and spiritual manner. By physical I mean you do things necessary to take care of yourself, your family, your body, and your mind. Spiritually you must give God's Kingdom work the highest priority. Let me reassure you—you are an ambassador. You are a representative of the Kingdom of God. You represent the government of Heaven. You can even legislate (bind and loose) on behalf of the Kingdom. So, what are you binding? What are you loosing? Your voice has tremendous power and authority because you represent the higher Kingdom. Therefore, when you speak the Word of the Lord by faith, Heaven responds. When you pray for your nation or your government or your leaders, stand in your role as ambassador, agree with Heaven, and watch these areas and individuals change. Death and life are in the power of your tongue (Proverbs 18:21). What are you speaking? What are you praying? In these last days, the Lord is looking for radical believers. Those who will take Him at His word no matter what. He's looking for those who understand their Kingdom mandate. You have the Spirit of God living within you! There is nothing you cannot do because you "can do all things through Christ" (Philippians 4:13).

An ambassador is not timid because he/she operates in the strength of the Lord and according to the power given to them by the Lord. Everything

God wants to do through you has already been prepared for you! Release the God within and let Him take you to higher heights. Walk in complete freedom. Dare to be different. Remove yourself from hope robbers and dream snatchers. Robe yourself in your ambassadorial authority and set your heart to hear how the Lord desires to move through you. Start releasing decrees on behalf of Heaven and change your life, family, job, schools, churches, and governments, for the better!

CHAPTER EIGHT

Walk in Your Kingdom Authority and Win!

> "But you shall receive power when the Holy Spirit has come upon you; and you shall be witnesses to Me in Jerusalem, and in all Judea and Samaria, and to the end of the earth."
> Acts 1:8

If you're reading this book and have been a believer for some time and feel you have wasted quite a bit of time on menial pursuits, it's not too late to hit the reset button. If you haven't been taught about who you are in the Kingdom of God, now's the time to hit the launch button. If you have stepped away from God because you felt this Christian journey was much too difficult, now's your time to hit the reset button. If you have been tossed and turned with the cares of this life and have become weary in your service to the Lord, hit that reset button NOW!

You serve a loving Father who knows you better than you could ever know yourself. His ultimate desire for you is intimacy with Him. He desires nothing more than to fellowship with you and to communicate His heart to you. As you draw near to Him, you will begin to hear His still small voice speaking to you. He will give some of you dreams and show you visions and communicate in various ways. He will guide you through His Word and you will begin to encounter Him more. The King Himself reveals your Kingdom identity. He knows every intricate detail about you. Do you not think the God of the Universe knows what to do with your children or your spouse or your place of employment? Everything you have is a gift from Him and He desires to show you HOW to manage and steward what He has given you.

You have discovered throughout this book how Jesus really sees you, and now He wants you to push that reset button so that you can be who you really are! Your identity may have been stolen or hidden for a short time due to life situations or maybe even due to a lack of understanding, but now is the time to awaken the real you and launch forward into your purpose. Every day, begin to tell yourself that you are a son, a king, a priest and an ambassador of the Most High God. Ask yourself if you are praying like a king and priest. This is an awareness that you should live in everyday. When you pray, pray from the position of a son and a priest. When you're praying for things to come into agreement with God's Word, pray from the position of a king. A king is never concerned about whether his decree will be carried out. The bible says that when you ask, you receive. When I approach Abba Father from the position and mindset of a son, I have the Father's attention because of my legal position as his son. Because of Jesus, you have been given various forms and levels of authority with various jurisdictions. To church leaders, when you meet resistance when attempting to achieve God's goals in the church, pray from your position of ambassador. You have legal, spiritual jurisdiction over your congregations and various locations. Pray from that position of authority, line up with the will of Heaven, and look for results! When Paul commissioned believers in Ephesians 6 to put on the whole armor of God, was he speaking of literal military armor? No! He was talking figuratively about spiritual things and spiritual armor and how you protect yourself in order do battle. For example, in the spirit, you must be robed with the righteousness of Jesus Christ which means you don't approach the Father in your own righteousness, only in the righteousness of Christ. Truth must be worn as your belt and the Word of God is your sword.

Jesus has already defeated the enemy for you. The only thing you have to do is walk in the victory already obtained! Why fight a battle that's already won? What you do as a believer is remind the enemy that he has already been defeated and because you are seated with Christ in Heavenly places NOW, you are victorious. Jesus promised every believer in Acts 1:5 a baptism in the Holy Spirit. This baptism is different from that of John the Baptist's baptism that focused on repentance. This baptism deals with the endowment of power or an ability or might to carry out the plan and purposes of the Father. This dunamis or strength is internal and emanates from Holy Spirit. This same power gave the apostles the ability to perform miracles, to gain influence, to live in moral excellence, and to witness with maximum effectiveness. The authority to operate in this power came from the Father as a promise to the every believer. This authority to walk in the power of Holy Spirit was not only given to the apostles. No, this same power is also available for you and me. The ministry of the Kingdom of God will only be accomplished by the power of Holy Spirit.

The Word that came to Zerubbabel in Zechariah 4:6b was, "Not by might nor by power, but by My Spirit, Says the LORD of hosts." It is Holy Spirit who provides the anointing and power to carry out your various assignments. It will not be in your human strength, ability, intellect, or influence that will fulfill the plan of God; it will be the power of Holy Spirit.

So, permission has been granted for you to do Kingdom business. My purpose for writing this book is to bring you into an awareness of your true identity in Christ Jesus so that you can understand the power you have in fulfilling your Kingdom assignment. The local church has need of the gifts placed within you. Because of who you are in the Kingdom, you should be walking in a higher level of influence than that of non-believers. You should be hearing the voice of God with clarity. You should be making impact and a difference in your various ministries, marketplaces, communities and countries. Those around you should be able to see a difference in how you live, how you talk, and the grace you walk in. As a son of God, you have a royal, eternal inheritance. As a king, you have rulership and governmental rights and authority. When you pray from the place of a king, you are able to declare and decree by faith. You have the power to decree healing in your family, mental stability, success on your job and in your business. As a king, find out your purpose and partner with God to see its fulfillment. Whatever the Lord has spoken over your life, don't allow one minor detail of that Word to fall to the ground. As a priest, you can intercede on behalf of God's people in the Name of Jesus and watch their lives change. As His priest, you can intercede for others and the prayer of faith, your faith, will save the sick.

      As an ambassador of Jesus Christ, you serve as His representative on earth. You say what He says. You represent the Kingdom and its standards. You are an official here to serve the King's people by enacting Kingdom principles. You have been called to function in all of these roles. Your victory lies within your ability to operate in your Kingdom role. Your identity is who you really are according to God. There's an awareness that you must awaken to in order to fully "take your mountain." To become aware of something means to come into the knowledge or understanding and this knowledge should cause a change in your perception. Perception has to do with the ability to see and/or hear and understand something or a thing. Now that you see and perceive yourself as a true son, priest, king and ambassador, begin to pray and live your life as such. Your position has everything to do with where Christ has placed you in His Kingdom and it is from this position that you engage Heaven in order to see victory for you, your family, and His Kingdom.

    We are living in very volatile times. Our religious freedoms are slowly being diminished and our identities threatened. Because of our holistic belief in the Bible, we are being viewed as fanatics and non-inclusive. It's funny how Christianity is the main religion under attack these days. So with that being said, this is not the time to be timid, my sisters and brothers. This is not the time to be reluctant or ignorant. The Lord said in Hosea 4:6a, "My people are destroyed for lack of knowledge." You know who you are now. To live beneath any of the roles granted to you by Jesus could result in living as a servant rather than a son.

    You MUST agree with God about who you are....even if you don't feel like a king today. I'm sure Jesus didn't feel like a king when He was being spat upon or feeling the pain and trauma of His skin being ripped apart by the whip of a cat-o'-nine-tails, or the agonizing separation from His Father on that demeaning cross. However, He was just as much the King then as He is now! Your current situation does not dictate your eternal status. Who you are in God is not contingent upon your myopic view of yourself. Your emotions don't define who you are. As a matter of fact, your emotions do a great job at distorting the real you because emotions are governed by day-to-day occurrences, situations, and feelings that change like the wind. This is why you can be happy one minute and irate the next. Here's how James, the brother of Jesus, puts it in his epistle (James 1:8). James warns that a double-minded man is unstable in all his ways. To be double-minded means to be wavering, uncertain, and doubting. To avoid living as one with two minds, you must set a firm foundation of faith. You cannot allow people, circumstances, sickness, status, the love of money and various other things to define you. Even without money, you are a son, king, priest, and ambassador. Even without a title or fame, you are still a son, king, priest, and ambassador of God Most High.

When you take the time to sit in the presence of the Lord and scribe what Holy Spirit is saying to you, you are spending time with Heaven. When you take the time to be intentional about meditating on the scriptures and allowing the Word to saturate your spirit man, you are engaging with Heaven. When you praise and worship and saturate your environment with spiritual songs, you are engaging with Heaven. When you sing to the Lord or dance or play before Him, you are engaging Heaven and when you engage with Heaven, Heaven responds and you will gain Heavenly insights.

When I began my journey as a worship leader, I had no idea of the places that Holy Spirit would take me. I knew that I loved God and wanted to be in His presence every opportunity that I could. I would spend hours in the Word and studying. I would ask Holy Spirit to illuminate my understanding of the scriptures and ask how to apply them to my everyday life. I became thirsty for Jesus. There was a passion and stirring within me that would settle for nothing less than an encounter with Him. As a result of my pursuit, my spiritual eyes began to open, and I could see and discern spiritual things. My spiritual ears opened, and I could hear the voice of the Spirit with clarity. All of these things happened because I was intentional, and not only did I attend a church that welcomed the gifts of the Spirit, they also provided the freedom to operate in those gifts. I was hungry for the Bread of Life. As I lead worship, I would always envision myself ministering before the Throne of God. The more I would do this, the heavier the anointing became. There was also an intensity and fervor that accompanied my worship. Because the Lord had allowed me to experience His wonderful peace and joy that flowed from His presence, I learned how to avoid distractions that could cause me to miss His presence. I learned how to take my eyes off people and fix them on Jesus. I became a master jeweler, always on the lookout for the priceless nuggets and jewels I could only find when being in His presence. I developed an insatiable longing for more of Jesus that only He could satisfy. He became the object of my affection and this chasing after HIM has radically changed my life forever.

Your mind can be your greatest asset or your greatest detriment. If satan can keep you confused about your place and role in the Kingdom, then your destiny will never be realized. It's amazing how they say that if you can do something consistently for seven days, you can change a habit. You can get rid of an old habit by enacting a new habit in its place for seven consecutive days. This practice has everything to do with renewing the mind so that the behavior will follow. When you start your day with the Lord, allow the Word of God to define who you are. Embrace what it says, and implement it into your day-to-day life. You my friend, will begin to change the course of your life! The currency of the Kingdom is faith, and when you agree with the Word in faith, transformation and awakening happens.

Every Word of God will breathe life into any dead situation or environment. What you think determines what you say, and what you say determines how you live. When you pray, begin to release the words to God with authority. When you sing or play or preach or teach, do it from a place of victory and authority. Boldness has everything to do with confidence in God, not shouting at the top of your lungs. Authority has already been granted to you, and earth is your jurisdiction. Jesus often astounded the Pharisees and Sadducees and religious leaders because of His wisdom and knowledge, and they were constantly asking where He received His authority.

As a Kingdom citizen, you manage the affairs of the Kingdom when you equip the saints for the work of the ministry and edify the body of Christ (Ephesians 1:4:12). One of the responsibilities I have includes teaching and training minstrels and psalmist. Because I understand my role as priest in this responsibility, I can guide my team through the spiritual paths of leading worship from a spiritual place instead of an earthly one. When we encounter places or people of resistance, through the guidance of Holy Spirit, I teach them how to use their voices, instruments and hands as weapons of praise unto God. As you align yourself with your respective purpose, the Lord will give you strategies for how to complete His work.

There is greatness inside of every person reading this book. The Lord has crafted you into a beautifully complex spirit being and placed you in a human body with divine purpose written in your DNA. There are people waiting on you to release what God has stored inside of you. There are hidden gifts inside of you and all you need is a Word from Holy Spirit to help revolutionize you and catapult you into your new season. Abba wants to release businesses and creativity to and through you. You are pregnant with purpose and Holy Spirit is ready to launch you into that purpose.

You may be familiar with the seven mountains of influence in that many people believe we have been called to serve in some capacity. In case you have never heard of them, they are the mountains of: Religion, Family, Government, Arts and Entertainment, Education, Media and Business. As the church of Jesus Christ and as a born-again believer, you should possess a great level of influence on at least one of these mountains. Everyone can rule on the mountain of family. You must follow the teachings of the Bible regarding family and refute anything that tries to sabotage the sanctity of the family. As I have also mentioned in a previous chapter, some of the agendas that are lurking before us today have absolutely NOTHING to do with love, but all have to do with the destruction of the family as God ordained it. It is Satan's plight to pervert what God has called holy and sanctified. (I won't take the time to go through the seven mountains of influence individually, but it is important to know which area Jesus has called you to influence. There are many of you with marketplace [business] mandates who are called to manage businesses and to lead with integrity, honesty and a servant's heart, so now's your time.)

Abandonment to Jesus is what this book calls for! That's what it's going to take to walk in your true identity in the days ahead. You must continue to grow in Him. Jesus said in John 15:4 that the branch cannot bear fruit apart from the vine. You are the extended branches intimately connected to the vine, Jesus Christ, and you gain your life and substance from Him. The branches do not tell the vine what to do. As long as the branches stay connected, they sustain life and bear fruit. You cannot do exploits for the Lord apart from abiding in Jesus and allowing His life to cause your life to bear fruit for the Kingdom. You are already equipped with everything you need to carry out your assignment. Your personality, your gifts, your stature; everything has been tailor-made inside of you to assist you in fulfilling your destiny.

During a recent early morning Sunday worship service, Pastor Turkington talked about making an impact. He said, "You may not impact the whole world, but you can impact your world." I find it very fascinating that true believers honestly want to make an indelible impact for God, but oftentimes don't have the encouragement or wisdom to move forward to carry out what's in their hearts. God has placed something inside of you that He wants to manifest through you. Wow! Abba Father strategically placed gifts and callings and abilities within you because He wants to demonstrate Himself through you. Once you yield to the purposes of Christ, He will accomplish that purpose through His Spirit, His power, and His might, according to His time. How do you think Sampson had the strength he possessed? It was Holy Spirit's might upon him (the Spirit of might-Isaiah 11:2).

    Refuse to allow the spirit of fear to talk you out of your purpose, and the spirit of deception to deceive you regarding your identity. You are God's secret weapon and He has need of you. You are a diamond in the rough waiting to be put on display! You are His warrior bride ready for battle! You are an arrow in His bow ready to be launched.

    My prayer is that you discover the importance of your identity and are ready to walk in that identity. When you lead worship, lead worship from your position as priest. Intercessors and watchman, when you pray, pray from your position as priest. As you carry out day-to-day ministry, do so from your kingly position. Be like David and approach your Goliaths with boldness and confidence in the Lord your God. The enemy has no legal right to hold back anything you own or anything connected to you once you have confessed. Whatever you declare unlawful, Heaven will declare unlawful, and whatever you loose or declare lawful, Heaven will do the same. Put on the mind of Christ. Ask Jesus to let you think as He thinks. Ask Holy Spirit to open your spiritual eyes so that you can see Kingdom realities more clearly.

    Arise, mighty warrior! It's time to fulfill your destiny. You have a beautiful identity in Christ. You have waited long enough. Go out and impact your world. Souls are waiting for you. Families and communities need your business, gifts and ideas. The homeless need your encouragement. They need your smile. They need your expertise. The widows need your love! You are God's best-kept secret! No more feeling inept. You have all you need inside of you. Take that first step of faith and begin to believe in yourself. There's nobody like you, and no one can do what you do. You are a son of God! You are a king! You are a priest! You are an ambassador and you have the Spirit of the Living God living inside of you. So walk in your true Kingdom identity with assurance, courage, and with godly authority. You were created to win so go and live your life in total victory!

PRAYER OF ACTIVATION

Father, in the Name of Your Holy and precious Son Jesus, the Messiah, I pray a prayer of impartation for everyone reading this book. I ask Holy Spirit that You reveal his/her purpose in this season. I ask that You awaken a passion within them to see Your purpose fulfilled through them.

YOU PRAY:
Father, I repent for allowing the opinions of others to cause me to live beneath my privileges. Father, I also repent for wrong mindsets regarding your identity. I ask that stolen identities be returned in Jesus' Name.

Holy Spirit I ask that You give me fresh revelation of the Word and what it says about me. I declare today that I will no longer see myself from a carnal and earthly viewpoint, but from a Heavenly one. I ask that the blood of Jesus cover my heart and protect me from deception about who I am and the authority I possess. I thank You, Lord, that You have given me everything that pertains to life and godliness. I declare that I am fearfully and wonderfully made in Your image. I thank You, Lord, that I am not an afterthought, but I am a God-thought. I thank You, Lord that I have purpose written in my DNA, and I am not defeated. I thank You that I am Your son; I am Your king seated in Jesus; I am Your priest and Your ambassador; I am Your bride and You are my Lord. From this day forward, I remove the old wineskins of self-doubt, and I put on the new wineskins of a transformed mind.

Your Identity in Christ

Today I choose to live the ascended life. I choose to walk close with You. Today I choose to be a steward of Your Word and guard my heart. I declare that no weapon formed against me shall prosper and every tongue that rises up against me in judgment, I will condemn because this is my heritage. I decree that all things are working together for my good because I am the called of God. I thank You, Father, that today I see myself through the lenses of scripture. I declare that greater is He that is in me than He that is in the world. I declare that I am more than a conqueror through Christ Jesus, and I win. I declare that I am going to live, operate and function in my Kingdom roles every day of my life. I love You, Lord, and my highest honor is to serve You and be a part of Your Kingdom agenda. I thank You that You're giving me a heart for Your people. I declare that I will serve Your people, my family, my community, my government, and my business as You are leading me, and I will do so with a spirit of integrity and excellence. Jesus, I know You are soon to return, so I pray that I am found doing the works that You have laid aside for me with a heart of gratitude and a spirit of grace and humility.

These things I pray in Jesus' Name. Amen.

REFERENCES

1. Myles, Dr. Francis. (2013). The Consciousness of NOW. Arlington, TX: Order of Melchizedek Holdings (in partnership with) The Order of Leadership University AKA OMLU/NIC.

2. Jim Springer (2016). What is DNA. Retrieved from <http://lifehopeandtruth.com/god/is-there-a-god/intelligent-design/dna/>.

3. National Human Genome Research Institute (June 16, 2015). Deoxyribonucleic Acid (DNA). Retrieved from <https://www.genome.gov/25520880>.

4. "H1564 - golem - Strong's Hebrew Lexicon (NKJV)." Blue Letter Bible. Web. 6 May, 2016. <https://www.blueletterbible.org//lang/lexicon/lexicon.cfm?Strongs=H1564&t=NKJV>.

5. "H5612 - cepher - Strong's Hebrew Lexicon (NKJV)." Blue Letter Bible. Web. 6 May, 2016. <https://www.blueletterbible.org//lang/lexicon/lexicon.cfm?Strongs=H5612&t=NKJV>.

6. "G3306 - menō - Strong's Greek Lexicon (KJV)." Blue Letter Bible. Web. 11 Jul, 2016. <https://www.blueletterbible.org//lang/lexicon/lexicon.cfm?Strongs=G3306&t=KJV>.

7. "H3789 - kathab - Strong's Hebrew Lexicon (NKJV)." Blue Letter Bible. Web. 6 May, 2016. <https://www.blueletterbible.org//lang/lexicon/lexicon.cfm?Strongs=H3789&t=NKJV>.

8. "H3117 - yowm - Strong's Hebrew Lexicon (NKJV)." Blue Letter Bible. Web. 6 May, 2016. <https://www.blueletterbible.org//lang/lexicon/lexicon.cfm?Strongs=H3117&t=NKJV>.

9. "H3335 - yatsar - Strong's Hebrew Lexicon (NKJV)." Blue Letter Bible. Web. 6 May, 2016. <https://www.blueletterbible.org//lang/lexicon/lexicon.cfm?Strongs=H3335&t=NKJV>.

10. "G2980 - laleō - Strong's Greek Lexicon (NKJV)." Blue Letter Bible. Web. 16 May, 2016. <https://www.blueletterbible.org//lang/lexicon/lexicon.cfm?Strongs=G2980&t=NKJV>.

11. Deny--"G533 - aparneomai - Strong's Greek Lexicon (NKJV)." Blue Letter Bible. Web. 14 Jul, 2016. <https://www.blueletterbible.org//lang/lexicon/lexicon.cfm?Strongs=G533&t=NKJV>.

12. "G1381 - dokimazō - Strong's Greek Lexicon (NKJV)." Blue Letter Bible. Web. 12 Jul, 2016. <https://www.blueletterbible.org//lang/lexicon/lexicon.cfm?Strongs=G1381&t=NKJV>.

13. Whiston, Thomas. The Works of Josephus: New Updated Edition; Complete and Unabridged in One Volume. Hendrickson Publishers, Inc. 1987. Page 35.

14. Led--"G71 - agō - Strong's Greek Lexicon (NKJV)." Blue Letter Bible. Web. 2 Jul, 2016. <https://www.blueletterbible.org//lang/lexicon/lexicon.cfm?Strongs=G71&t=NKJV>.

15. Adoption--"G5206 - huiothesia - Strong's Greek Lexicon (NKJV)." Blue Letter Bible. Web. 2 Jul, 2016. <https://www.blueletterbible.org//lang/lexicon/lexicon.cfm?Strongs=G5206&t=NKJV>.

16. Sons-"G5207 - huios - Strong's Greek Lexicon (NKJV)." Blue Letter Bible. Web. 2 Jul, 2016. <https://www.blueletterbible.org//lang/lexicon/lexicon.cfm?Strongs=G5207&t=NKJV>.

17. Kings-"G935 - basileus - Strong's Greek Lexicon (NKJV)." Blue Letter Bible. Web. 2 Jul, 2016. <https://www.blueletterbible.org//lang/lexicon/lexicon.cfm?Strongs=G935&t=NKJV>.

18. Bind-"G1210 - deō - Strong's Greek Lexicon (KJV)." Blue Letter Bible. Web. 2 Jul, 2016. <https://www.blueletterbible.org//lang/lexicon/lexicon.cfm?Strongs=G1210&t=KJV>.

www.ingramcontent.com/pod-product-compliance
Lightning Source LLC
LaVergne TN
LVHW051500070426
835507LV00022B/2849